STYLES for ENGLISH LANGUAGE

Developing Techniques in Prose, Drama and Verse

STYLES for ENGLISH LANGUAGE

Developing Techniques in Prose, Drama and Verse

SIDNEY R. THOMAS, B.A.

BLANDFORD PRESS
Poole   Dorset

First published in the U.K. 1979

Copyright © 1979 Blandford Press Ltd,
Link House, West Street,
Poole, Dorset BH15 1LL

British Library Cataloguing in Publication Data
Thomas, Sidney R
    Styles for English language.
    1. English literature – Study and teaching
    (Secondary) – Great Britain
    2. English language – Style
    I. Title
    820'.9   PR51.G7
    ISBN 0 7137 1018 7 (Hardback edition)
        0 7137 1037 3 (Limp edition)

Set in 11/12 pt Apollo by Keyspools Ltd, Golborne, Lancs.
Printed in Great Britain by Fakenham Press Ltd, Norfolk.

CONTENTS

TO THE TEACHER

This book is not an English course which has to be followed slavishly from beginning to end. Its *main* aim is to present pupils with a considerable number of varied ideas to help them to improve their writing skills. The exercises provide practice for candidates preparing for examinations in C.S.E. and in G.C.E. to 'O' Level. Non-examination pupils should also find a good deal of stimulative material.

Formal work included concentrates on those areas in which pupils appear to experience most difficulty.

ACKNOWLEDGEMENTS

The author and publisher are grateful for permission to quote extracts from the following:

HATTER'S CASTLE by A. J. Cronin (Victor Gollancz Ltd.)
LORD OF THE FLIES by William Golding (Faber and Faber Ltd.)
GALE WARNING from *COLLECTED POEMS* by Michael Roberts (Faber and Faber Ltd.)
THE DAY OF THE TRIFFIDS by John Wyndham (Michael Joseph Ltd.)
A STORY from *A PROSPECT OF THE SEA AND OTHER STORIES* by Dylan Thomas (reprinted by permission of the Trustees for the Copyrights of the late Dylan Thomas and J. M. Dent & Sons Ltd.)
THE BOY WHO WAS AFRAID by Armstrong Sperry (The Bodley Head)
SLOWLY from *THE WANDERING MOON* by James Reeves (William Heinemann Ltd.)
CIDER WITH ROSIE by Laurie Lee (The Hogarth Press.)
NOTTINGHAM AND THE MINING COUNTRYSIDE from *PHOENIX* by D. H. Lawrence (reprinted by permission of Laurence Pollinger Limited and the Estate of the late Mrs Frieda Lawrence Ravagli; Pub: William Heinemann Ltd.)
A SOUND OF THUNDER by Ray Bradbury (reprinted by permission of A. D. Peters and Co. Ltd.; Pub: Hart-Davis)
THE CRUEL SEA by Nicholas Monsarrat (Cassell and Co. Ltd.)

Photographs are reproduced by kind permission of the following: Peter Baker, pp 34, 76, 111, 149; Central Office of Information (Crown copyright reserved), p 133; Committee for Aerial Photography, University of Cambridge, p 67; *Farmers Weekly*, p 65; Hong Kong Government Information Services (Crown copyright reserved), p 136; Volkswagen, p 155; and the author, pp 23, 47, 96, 117, 153.

1 THE WRITER AND HIS SENSES

It is fair to assume that everyone likes stories of one sort or another. Whatever the choice, all tales have certain common 'ingredients'! For example, every story requires *characters* (human or otherwise). A tale has to happen in some *place*, against some kind of *background*. Then, any good story must contain a certain amount of *suspense*. Something has to *happen*. That is, there must be some kind of *action* – and the whole should lead up to a *climax*.

We realise that writers have to be skilled in the use of words and that they need to know and use a wide *vocabulary*. They must also employ their *imaginations*. So much is obvious. What does not appear to be so obvious, especially amongst young writers in school, is that authors must also use their *senses*.

Read the following passage, taken from an exciting book – *The Day of the Triffids*. The narrator is in hospital, recovering from an operation. He wakes one morning with the feeling that all is not well.

But this morning was different. Disturbingly because mysteriously different. No wheels rumbled, no buses roared, no sound of a car of any kind, in fact, was to be heard. No brakes, no horns, not even the clopping of the few rare horses that still occasionally passed. Nor, as there should be at such an hour, the composite tramp of work-bound feet.

The more I listened, the queerer it seemed – and the less I cared for it. In what I reckoned to be ten minutes of careful listening I heard five sets of shuffling, hesitating footsteps, three voices bawling unintelligibly in the distance, and the hysterical sobs of a woman. There was not the cooing of a pigeon, not the chirp of a sparrow. Nothing but the humming of wires in the wind. . . .

A nasty, empty feeling began to crawl up inside me. It was the same sensation I used to have sometimes as a child when I got to fancying that horrors were lurking in the shadowy corners of the bedroom; when I daren't put a foot out for fear that something should reach from under the bed and grab my ankle; daren't even reach for the switch lest the movement should cause something to leap at me. I had to fight down the feeling, just as I had to when I was a kid in the dark. And it was no easier. . . .

From *The Day of the Triffids* by **John Wyndham**

In that extract the author has concentrated on his sense of *hearing* and his sense of *feeling*. You should also notice that *suspense* is created immediately.

Think of yourself and of your own senses for a moment. Your eyes allow you to *see* beautiful views, scenes of desolation, dangerous situations and so on. Your sense of *smell* can give you pleasure in a garden of flowers, or in a chip shop on a cold winter evening. It can warn you of danger when there is a gas leak. You *touch* a hot iron and know that to pick it up would be foolish and painful. In a large shop the heat might be unbearable and you *feel* faint and know that you must return to the cool air outside. A meat pie that is unsafe to eat will reveal itself to your sense of *taste*.

A blind carpenter had a workshop full of sharp tools, but there were no light switches on the walls. The fact that there were no lights appeared strange only to the visitor with sight. Can you imagine finding your way about in that place – *and* producing an article of furniture?

It is difficult, if not impossible, to imagine living without our senses. Does it not seem strange, then, to write about characters who appear to enjoy the use of just one or two senses?

Whatever you write – remember your senses.

Read the following passages:

a SEEING

Where once had stood the great city there was now devastation. Gigantic blocks of flats had collapsed into massive heaps of smoking rubble. Water, gushing from a hundred ruptured pipes, sparkled in hissing jets high in the air. Buses, lorries, cars lay flattened beneath colossal pillars which had been hurled through the fevered atmosphere like sticks of straw before a winnowing wind. On the far horizon huge clouds of reddened smoke struggled to blot out the sun.

b TASTING

He tried to lick his blackened lips, but his swollen tongue refused to move. Ice! His mind returned again and again to ice. He thought of it melting and the chilled water trickling, cool and sweet, down his arid throat, freezing in his stomach. He recalled summer days, long past, when he lay in the shade of the oak tree at the end of the village street, soaking his mouth in sharp lemonade, bitter lime or sickly-sweet orange concoctions. What wouldn't he give for one of those slim, tall glasses, light with frothy bubbles, heavy with liquid? Liquid! Any liquid! He raised his eyes once more to peer over the shimmering desert, the baked rocks. Ice! Ice! Ice!

The extracts concentrate on *two* of the senses. Write other passages which concentrate on *hearing, feeling* and *smelling*.

Having done that, compose a passage where several of the senses are utilised.

Dramatic Movement

To stimulate your imagination and to give you the 'feel' of your *senses* the following might be useful. Perhaps your teacher will read the instructions while you perform.

a Individual work

Move freely and react quickly to these suggestions. Between each 'reaction' return to free movement such as running, skipping, walking.

1 You are walking in the park when you *see* something amusing.
2 You *see* something puzzling.
3 You *hear* a strange sound.
4 Something frightens you.
5 You hide quickly and watch.

b Work in pairs

1 Stand across the room, opposite your partner. Walk towards each other and imagine that you are friends who meet unexpectedly after many years.
2 Two people who dislike one another meet.
3 Now the two people find one another extremely funny.
4 Two people who terrify one another at sight.

c More Individual work

Listen to the following story and act it as it is being told:

You are lying on a sandy beach after having been washed ashore during the night. It is now early morning and you are alone – asleep.

Slowly you wake. You *feel* the hot sun on your back. You sit up and realise that you appear to be alone in a strange place. You *look* around, but you see no one. Now you *feel* thirsty, hungry and a little nervous.

You rise and stretch your stiff muscles. (You have not injured yourself on the rocks, have you? You had better check.) Now *move* into the forest. You *hear* strange noises. Move on. You *see* some fruit. It *smells* good. *Taste* it!

Back to the beach you go where the mid-day sun is very hot. You must find some shelter and sleep again.

Suddenly you are awakened by the sounds of wild creatures. Make a fire and build a crude shelter.

You *hear* someone approach. Hide and keep very still.

Someone is approaching. First you *hear* him. Now you *see* him. He looks harmless. Come out from your hiding-place . . . carefully. You distrust the newcomer, but he makes it obvious that he is very glad to see you. You make friends – sharing your food and water with him.

Working in groups, discuss the following ideas and then try to perform them. Concentrate on action where you use your *senses*:

1 Mime another scene on an island.
2 Try the scene again – making up some dialogue.
3 Improvise a scene involving people – at a market, on board a ship, at the seaside.
4 A group of people wade across a river which is fast-flowing and full of crocodiles.
5 A group of friends try to find the way out of an underground cave.

Make the scenes busy and real. Perhaps each group would like to perform while the rest of the class watches.

2 PEOPLE

How did you come to school this morning?

However you came, it is fairly safe to assume that you met *people*. In the class-room you are surrounded by *people*. There are *people* at home, at the cinema, on television.

When you are first introduced to someone what do you notice first – hands, eyes, nose? When he has gone can you remember him well enough to describe him? How would you describe your postman, for example? He is of average height. He has fair hair and is clean-shaven. How good is that description?

Here is a description of a person, not your postman, but someone:

He was a short man, a very short, squat individual who never walked. He waddled at high speed, his great bag of letters bouncing off his ample hips. The most noticeable aspect of his appearance, however, was the long, brown mackintosh which flapped against his calves – whatever the weather. It was said that only in the hottest of summers did he leave the coat at home. We never witnessed such occasions. The hat, which rested somewhat precariously on his wide head, reminded us of those we had seen in pictures of savage sea captains, but there was nothing savage about him. His round face, under a weather-beaten tan, was smooth and youthful, his mouth set permanently in a gentle smile and his blue eyes always bright.

Notice that the description is not merely a catalogue of his physical appearance . . . blue eyes, fair hair, wide shoulders and so on.

See how well you can write a description of someone who calls regularly at your house, or someone you often see in the street.

Do you remember this nursery-rhyme?

> Humpty Dumpty sat on a wall!
> Humpty Dumpty had a great fall!
> All the king's horses and all the king's men
> Couldn't put Humpty together again.

From those four lines only can you describe Humpty Dumpty? Like an egg! Why would you say that? Probably because you have seen pictures of him like that.

Read the following:

Bill Smith sat on a wall!
Bill Smith had a great fall!
All the doctors, both women and men
Failed to put Bill together again.

Can you *describe* Bill Smith? Why not? What do you need to know about a character in order to make him 'real'? Here are some ideas:

a Physical appearance
1 Is he tall, short, fat, thin, old, young?
2 Describe his hair, eyes, mouth, shape of face, beard etc.
3 Are there any unusual marks on his face – a scar, a mole?
4 Does he limp? Has he a lisp? Has he a finger missing?
b Personality
1 Has he any particular associates? e.g. policemen, thieves, artists, sportsmen?
2 Has he any hobbies such as fishing, dancing, flying, climbing?
3 Is he friendly or does he keep himself to himself?
4 Does he go to theatres, football matches, cycle races?
5 Does he keep pets?
6 Is he a kindly sort of person?
7 Do other people like him?
8 What do others say and think about him?
9 How does he behave when he is alone?
10 How does he behave in company?

Dramatic Movement

When you perform the following try to imagine that you are actually the people concerned. Think about how each would move.

a Individual work
Mime actions that might be performed by the following:
A king or queen.
A policeman.
A very old person.
An impatient middle-aged person waiting for a train.
A postman.
A fussy, talkative hair-dresser.

b Work in pairs
Invent dialogues between:
Two friends who have not seen each other for years.
A passenger and a 'bus-conductor.
A waitress and a diner.

A shop-keeper and a customer.
A policeman and a law-breaker.

c Work in groups

Improvise these scenes, inventing dialogue:
A group of strangers, or friends, travelling in a railway carriage.
Friends eating in a restaurant.
People in an open-air market.
A fancy-dress ball.
Patients in a doctor's waiting-room.
Performers waiting for work in the office of a theatrical agent.

Written Work

a. VOCABULARY

In order to make your writing really effective you will need a varied vocabulary. To give yourself a little practice make these lists of words:

1 Describing a person's eyes. (Colour, shape, size etc.)
2 Describing someone's hair. (Colour, amount, style etc.)
3 Describing how a person might speak. (Type of voice, manner of speaking etc.)
4 Describing how someone moves. (Clothes, equipment carried, age of person – all will have some effect on movement)
5 Describing how a person might feel. (Exhausted, happy etc.)

b READ THE FOLLOWING:

He was a tall, straight-backed man who had the appearance of someone who had known the discipline of military service. It was not only his urgent stride which made the suggestion. There was the close-cropped hair, the neatly-clipped greying moustache, the crisp manner of his speech – like that of a man accustomed to giving orders that were meant to be obeyed. . . .

That short description concentrates on physical details. He was 'tall', 'straight-backed'. He walked briskly. His hair was 'close-cropped', his moustache 'neatly-clipped'. Such details might enable us to recognise the man if we met him, but they do not tell us anything about him *as a man*, as a *person*.

Each evening, after she had finished her frugal tea, she sat in the corner of the ancient settee, knitting. She was always knitting, the nodding of her old white head seeming to match the steady rhythm of the clicking needles. Despite her industry, however, her own woollen garments were threadbare, but it was not difficult for the many friends who visited her to guess the reason why. The children of the village, snug in their crew-necks and polo-jumpers, were evidence of her skill and of her charity.

'Don't you ever stop knitting?' a small child had once asked.

'Lord, no,' chuckled the old woman. 'It keeps me young.'

'Keeps *you* young?'

'Course. It makes me contented, you see. And contentment keeps you young.'

And, indeed, she *was* young, for all her years. Her hair might be sparse, her face not free of wrinkles, her thin back no longer straight – but her dark eyes and gentle voice were fresh with the happiness of years past and remembered.

The second description differs from the first. How? Some physical features were mentioned; for example, the white hair, wrinkled face, dark eyes, gentle voice, bent back – but what else do we learn of the old woman?

She was contented. She was generous – giving away to the children the garments she made. Her great hobby was knitting – and we get the impression, although it was not stated, that she lived alone. The fact that she had many visitors tells us that she was well-liked.

Now read the following extracts:

1 THE OLD SEA DOG

I remember him as if it were yesterday, as he came plodding to the inn door, his sea-chest following behind in a hand-barrow; a tall, nut-brown man; his tarry pigtail falling over the shoulders of his soiled blue coat; his hands ragged and scarred, with black, broken nails; and the sabre cut across one cheek, a dirty livid white. I remember him looking round the cove and whistling to himself as he did so, and then breaking out in that old sea-song that he sang so often afterwards:

'Fifteen men on the dead man's chest –

Yo – ho – ho, and a bottle of rum!'

in the high, old tottering voice that seemed to have been tuned and broken at the capstan bars. Then he rapped on the door with a bit of a stick like a hand-spike that he carried, and when my father appeared, called roughly for a glass of rum. This, when it was brought to him, he drank slowly, like a connoiseur, lingering on the taste, and still looking about him at the cliffs and up at our sign-board.

'This is a handy cove,' says he, at length, 'and a pleasant sittyated grog-shop. Much company, mate?'

My father told him no, very little company, the more was the pity.

'Well, then,' said he, 'this is the berth for me. Here you, matey,' he cried to the man who trundled the barrow, 'bring up alongside and help up my chest. I'll stay here a bit,' he continued. 'I'm a plain man; rum and bacon and eggs is what I want, and that head up there for me to watch ships off. What you mought call me? You mought call me captain. Oh, I see what you're at – there,' and he threw down three or four gold pieces on the threshold. 'You can tell me when I've worked through that,' says he, looking as fierce as a commander.

And, indeed, bad as his clothes were and coarsely as he spoke, he had none of the appearance of a man who sailed before the mast; but seemed like a mate or skipper. . . .

From *Treasure Island* by **R. L. Stevenson**

From this passage – what do we learn about the old sea-dog?

a He was tall, strong, weather-beaten, scarred. His hands were rough and showed black, broken nails.

b His voice was high and tottering. He called roughly for a drink.

c He was a 'plain man' wanting only rum, bacon and eggs.

d He was probably not an ordinary seaman – 'but seemed like a mate or skipper'.

1 Explain why you think this man was pleased about the fact that very few people called at the inn.

2 There is something sinister about the old sea-dog. Describe what happened and how you reacted when he suddenly appeared on your doorstep.

2 UNCLE

In this extract we also learn something about 'auntie'.

I was staying at the time with my uncle and his wife. Although she was my aunt, I never thought of her as anything but the wife of my uncle, partly because he was so big and trumpeting and red-hairy and used to fill every inch of the hot little house like an old buffalo squeezed into an airing-cupboard, and partly because she was so small and silk and quick and made no noise at all as she whisked about on padded paws, dusting the china dogs, feeding the buffalo, setting the mousetraps that never caught her; and once she sleeked out of the room, to squeak in a nook or nibble in a hay loft, you forgot she had ever been there.

But there he was, always, a steaming hulk of an uncle, his bracers straining like hawsers, crammed behind the tiny counter of the shop at the front of the house, and breathing like a brass band; or guzzling and blustery in the kitchen over his gusty supper, too big for anything except the great black boats of his boots. As he ate, the house grew smaller; he billowed out over the furniture, the loud check meadow of his waistcoat littered, as though after a picnic, with cigarette ends, peeling, cabbage stalks, birds' bones, gravy. . . .

From *A Story* by **Dylan Thomas**

a What do you think 'uncle' was like as a person?

b What do you think 'auntie' was really like?

c Write a very short scene (as if part of a play) showing how uncle treated auntie.

d Write a piece of dialogue in which auntie is talking about uncle to a neighbour.

e Write a description of your favourite uncle or aunt.

3 THE MINERS

Now the colliers had also an instinct of beauty. The colliers' wives had not. The colliers were deeply alive, instinctively. But they had no daytime ambition, and no daytime intellect. They avoided, really, the rational aspect of life. They preferred to take life instinctively and intuitively. They didn't even care very profoundly about wages. It was the women, naturally, who nagged on this score. There was a big discrepancy, when I was a boy, between the collier who saw, at the best, only a few brief hours of daylight – often no daylight at all during the winter weeks – and the collier's wife, who had all the day to herself when the man was down pit.

The great fallacy is, to pity the man. He didn't dream of pitying himself, till agitators and sentimentalists taught him to. He was happy: or more than happy, he was fulfilled. Or he was fulfilled on the receptive side, not on the expressive. The collier went to the pub and drank in order to continue his intimacy with his mates. They talked endlessly, but it was rather of wonders and marvels, even in politics, than of facts. It was hard facts, in the shape of wife, money, and nagging home necessities, which they fled away from, out of the house to the pub, and out of the house to the pit.

The collier fled out of the house as soon as he could, away from the nagging materialism of the woman. With the woman it was always: This is broken, now you've got to mend it! or else: We want this, that and the other, and where is the money coming from? The collier didn't know and didn't care very deeply – his life was otherwise. So he escaped. He roved the countryside with his dog, prowling for a rabbit, for nests, for mushrooms, anything. He loved the countryside, just the indiscriminating feel of it. Or he loved just to sit on his heels and watch – anything or nothing. He was not intellectually interested. Life for him did not consist in facts, but in a flow. Very often he loved his garden, and very often he had a genuine love of the beauty of flowers. I have known it often and often in colliers.

Now the love of flowers is a very misleading thing. Most women love flowers as possessions, and as trimmings. They can't look at a flower, and wonder a moment, and pass on. If they see a flower that arrests their attention, they must at once pick it, pluck it. Possession! A possession! Something added on TO ME! And most of the so-called love of flowers today is merely this reaching out of possession and egoism: something I've GOT: something that embellishes ME. Yet I've seen many a collier stand in his back garden looking down at a flower with that odd, remote sort of contemplation which shows a real awareness of the presence of beauty. It would not even be admiration, or joy, or delight, or any of those things which so often have a root in the possessive instinct. It would be a sort of contemplation: which shows the incipient artists!

From *Nottingham and the Mining Countryside* by **D. H. Lawrence**

a Why do you think the miners craved for beauty?
b What do you think of the attitudes of the women? Can you

suggest any reasons why they wanted 'possessions'?

c Can you think of any other people who are deprived of beauty? Is beauty important to you?

4 THE POSTMAN

'He comes, the herald of a noisy world,
With spatter'd boots, strapp'd waist, and frozen locks;
News from all nations lumb'ring at his back.
True to his charge, the close-packed load behind,
Yet careless what he brings, his one concern
Is to conduct it to the destin'd inn:
And, having dropp'd th'expected bag, pass on.
He whistles as he goes, light-hearted wretch,
Cold and yet cheerful: messenger of grief
Perhaps to thousands, and joy to some;
To him indiff'rent whether grief or joy!

From *The Task* by **William Cowper**

People usually like receiving letters from others. Can you think of anyone who would like to receive a letter from you?

Now see what you can do. Write descriptions of the following. Mention some physical details, but introduce some aspects of 'character' as well:

a A pirate.
b A person who has spent some years alone on an island.
c A shop-keeper.
d A 'bus driver.
e A very old person.
f A tramp.
g A circus clown at home.
h A small child playing in the mud.
i An unusual relative.
j Yourself – as seen by your parents, yourself, or a friend.

Dialogue

Look at the following piece of conversation:

MARY (Meeting her friend, JUNE)
    Hello, June.
JUNE Hello, Mary.
MARY Nice day!
JUNE Mm. Better than yesterday.
MARY Been shopping?
JUNE Sort of.
MARY Sort of?
JUNE Well – I've been shopping, but bought nothing.

MARY Why not?

JUNE I couldn't see anything I wanted.

  (She shivers)

  It's not such a nice day after all.

What do you learn from that piece of conversation? That it is a pleasant day, though cold, that June has made an unsuccessful shopping expedition. That seems to be about all. Perhaps something interesting would be said if the dialogue continued, but everything written in a piece of conversation should be interesting and worth saying. Very often it should also indicate something about the character who is speaking, or the person being discussed.

Read the following:

MOTHER (Calling up the stairs)

  George! George! It's gone eight!

MARY Don't waste your breath, Mum. He won't miss his breakfast. He never does.

MOTHER Hmph! I can't see why he has to leave it to the last minute to get up.

MARY Well – you shouldn't let him read comics in bed.

MOTHER (A little annoyed)

  Me! *Let* him read! You try and stop him. Just you try.

MARY No thanks. His temper's too short for me. I pity any girl who's silly enough to marry him one day.

MOTHER (Moving to the foot of the stairs again)

  George!

MARY I wonder what he'll be like when he starts school!

What information do we find here? George is not yet five years of age, dislikes getting up in the morning, but enjoys his food. He is an avid reader of comics – and is a quick-tempered little boy.

Do we learn anything about the other characters? The mother appears to have little control over George – at least so far as his habit of lying in bed looking at comics is concerned.

Although we are given no indication as to the age of Mary we feel that she is considerably older than her brother and, even though she makes uncomplimentary remarks about him – she is probably very fond of him.

Write the following dialogues, being sure that you make the speakers say something interesting. If you can reveal something about the various characters as well so much the better.

a A policeman and a member of the public who is describing a missing relative. Choose your 'member of the public' carefully so that you can reveal something of him/her in the conversation, e.g. a forgetful old lady, or a man who likes to talk about himself.

b A 'bus conductor and a talkative passenger. You might locate this conversation on a quiet route in the country where the conductor might have time to listen, or on a busy city journey where he could easily become irate.

c A girl from long ago talks to a modern school-girl. You might call upon any knowledge you have gained from your History lessons to help you. Again, choose someone who lived a life very different from that of the modern girl, e.g. a mill girl of the nineteenth century, a Victorian housemaid etc.)

d A mother talks to her daughter about the latter's new boy-friend. The daughter will wish to present the boy's best qualities while the mother will ask some probing questions about his career prospects and so on.

OR Write the conversation which might take place between a father and his son who wishes to bring his girl-friend home.

e Two friends find a five pound note and try to decide what to do with it. Both might be dishonest enough to wish to keep it, or one might wish to hand it to the police, giving his reasons, while the other votes to keep it, also giving his reasons.

f A father talks to his son who wants to buy a motor-cycle. The father might be very cautious, pointing out the dangers attendant upon owning such a machine, the son being very keen to have one. Of course, the son will have to convince the father that he will be a careful and considerate driver.

g A teacher talks to a conscientious pupil who has suddenly stopped working. There could be a number of reasons for his/her action.

h Two competitors who are about to take part in some kind of contest talk to one another. They might be friends who will encourage one another, or they might be rivals who try to score some sort of 'psychological' advantage over each other. Do not let the conversation drift into a mere argument.

i A waitress in a cafe talks to a customer who has a complaint. Do not allow your customer to become abusive, nor your waitress 'superior'. There is a right way and a wrong way to make a complaint. Remember, too, that we all make mistakes.

j A housewife speaks to the milkman who is persistently late making his deliveries. You might make the milkman a person with a sense of humour. The housewife will have to give reasons why she requires the milk earlier than she is receiving it. Again, do not let the conversation develop into a quarrel.

Working in groups (Oral and/or written work)

a Two members of a club wish to introduce a new member, but some of the others object. Try to find good reasons why the proposed person should be accepted, and good reasons why he should not.

b Would-be mutineers meet secretly aboard ship. They will have to discuss their plans carefully and quickly – quickly in case they are disturbed and carefully because their plans must be successful.

c A school group try to choose (i) a School Captain, (ii) a games leader, (iii) a club leader.

d Several witnesses of a smash-and-grab raid describe to the police what they saw.

e Some members of a class try to decide who shall represent the form at an important function, e.g. a youth conference.

More ambitious group work

Write the following conversations. It might be helpful to 'perform' these first, making up some dialogue. Having done so, sit down together, decide what you really want to talk about and then write it out as a script before performing it again.

a A group of strangers are travelling on a train when they get into conversation. Avoid mere 'small talk' about the weather. Centre the conversation about one topic, e.g. holidays from which they are returning. Then see if you can make each person reveal something of herself/himself through her/his contribution to the dialogue. For example, one of the travellers might wish to proclaim that there is nowhere like London for a holiday, explaining why, whereas others might defend holidays abroad. Then there are caravan holidays, walking tours, seaside resorts.

b Some friends, who have been to a fun-fair, meet later in a cafe. Some will probably boast about the dangerous rides they enjoyed and the prizes they won. Plans for a next visit to the fair might be made. Some will even confess to having been nervous on some of the roundabouts and rides, perhaps. Then, of course, there could be some discussion about the refreshments they are to order.

c A group visit the waxworks and talk about some of the exhibits. Do not yield to the temptation to be silly here. This piece of dialogue could be made interesting if each speaker is able to provide some information about an exhibit.

d Some friends visit a large store to do their Christmas shopping.

Perhaps you might wish to make your speakers talk about presents they want to buy, for whom and why.

e A group of friends visit the Tower of London (or any other 'Tourist Attraction'). To do this well you should first read some informative material about the place of your choice so that you may make your speakers talk in an interesting and authoritative manner.

Letters

Here is an example:

56 Sundown Gardens,
Radlea,
Fernton.
30th April, 1978.

Dear Mary,

Thank you for your letter which arrived last week. Sorry I didn't answer sooner. We've been on holiday, which we didn't enjoy. It rained every day and it was freezing cold. Dad was the only one who liked it because he could go fishing whatever the weather was like. I would have gone round the shops, but there were only two in the village and they just sold groceries and newspapers.

While we were away I saw that Jimmy Phelps who used to bully everybody in school. I was glad when he left. He didn't see me. Thank goodness! Do you remember how he was always boasting that he was going to be an airline pilot? Then he was going to be a deep-sea diver. When I saw him he was working on the beach – giving out deck-chairs. Well, he would have been doing that if the sun had shone!

When we came home we found that somebody had broken into our house. They didn't steal much – just my brother's transistor radio and two of Dad's fishing cups. They left a mess, though. They had scribbled all over the walls and ripped the curtains downstairs. Mum was very upset, but she's a little better now. She said that she'll never go out of the house again.

I'm not looking forward to going back to school. Are you? We are having a new form-teacher. Maggie Smith said it's to be a man – a young man. I bet you wish you were in my class. Your Miss Lewis is a real dragon! Still – half-term's not too far away!

I must finish now because Mum wants me to help her with the shopping. Write soon.

Love,
June

Notice that the tone of the letter on page 15 is friendly, unlike the formal style used in business letters and essays. It is a 'conversational' style. Note, also, that shortened (contracted) forms (e.g. can't, I'm, hadn't) are used. Such contractions should not be used in formal English, but they are preferable when writing conversation because they make the composition sound more natural.

Most of us like to receive letters, and many of us dislike *writing* them, possibly because we cannot think of anything about which to write.

When composing a letter it is a good idea to imagine that you are actually *talking* to the person who is to receive it. You need not be as formal as you would be when writing, say, a report or an essay, but do not use slang if you can possibly manage without it.

Write a letter to a friend, making it as interesting as possible. Include several items such as

1 A description of a relative who has visited you.
2 Some information about a play you have seen.
3 Something new that you have bought.
4 An amusing photograph that you have taken.
5 A little about yourself.

Now write the following letters. The *main* items have been suggested in each case, with a little additional help in some cases.

a To a friend, describing an old beach-comber you met while on holiday. You might also include a paragraph describing some unusual excursion you enjoyed during your stay, and/or a new friend you made.

b To your parents, describing an interesting person you have met. You might be working in another town or village. If so, remember that your parents will want to know something about your welfare, your lodgings etc.

c A circus performer writes to a pen-friend, describing himself, his act, the kind of life he leads and the places he visits.

d To a friend, describing your new teacher.

e To a cousin, describing a distant relation who has come to pay you a long visit and who is causing life in your household to be somewhat 'chaotic'.

f Write to a difficult neighbour, apologising for the fact that your football has broken some of his flowers.

g Write a letter to a friend, asking his/her advice about some item that you wish to buy.

h Write to a friend, asking him/her to accompany you to a newly-formed club one evening.

i Write to a friend who was unsuccessful in the competition that you won.

j While you are on holiday write to a cousin, asking him/her to join you at the resort for a few days.

k Write to a neighbour, thanking her for inviting your small sister/brother to a party held to celebrate her child's birthday.

l An elderly relative has sent you some money for Christmas. Write to thank him/her, mentioning what you hope to do with the gift.

m Write to a sister who lives in another part of the country, congratulating her on the birth of her first baby.

n You have arranged to meet a friend at a particular place, but he/she fails to arrive. Write a (polite) letter, asking for an explanation.

o Now write the letter from the friend in answer to your inquiry.

p On behalf of your class, write a letter to your teacher who has had to retire prematurely.

q Write to your drama teacher, explaining why you have had to withdraw from taking part in the school play.

The following will be easier if you have heard about the people concerned during your History lessons. If you know little or nothing about them and you wish to write the letters then you might learn about them for yourself by looking up the information in reference books.

r Louis Pasteur was a chemist who discovered how animals and people might be protected against certain diseases by innoculation. Many people of his time, including doctors, refused to believe him. After you have finished your research (reading), or revised what you have learned in your lessons, write a series of letters that might pass between two people who discuss Pasteur, his work and conditions of life at the time, e.g. two doctors, one of whom believes in Pasteur and one who does not; Pasteur's wife and a friend; Pasteur and a disbelieving doctor.

s Elizabeth Fry lived many years ago when prisons in this country were, indeed, horrible places, where the inmates were kept in conditions worse than those endured by some animals. She faced much opposition to her ideas for reform. After you have done some useful research, write letters which might have passed between Elizabeth Fry and other people of her time – letters in which her ideas and prison conditions are discussed, e.g. members of the government of the day; prison governors; prisoners' wives.

t Many years ago the lives of a great many children were far from happy. Hundreds of boys and girls were put to work at a very early age in cotton-mills and coal-mines and many of them did not live to see the age of twelve. Such children had a champion, however, in the person of Lord Shaftesbury. When you have learned all you can about him and about the working conditions of such children, try to imagine yourself as being one of them and write a letter to your friend, describing your life and saying what you hope Lord Shaftesbury might be able to do to help you. Then write a letter from the friend to you. (This piece of work is artificial, of course, because if you really had been one of those unfortunate children you would have been unable to read or write.)

Formal letters

The following letters are different from those you have already written in that they are 'formal'. That means that they have certain rules governing their presentation and content. Look at this example:

                    A   56 Sundown Gardens,
                                 Radlea,
                               Fernton.
                    B   12th July, 1978.

The Personnel Manager,
C Lookrite Fashions Ltd.,
    1 Parkloft Road,
Férnton.

D Dear Sir,

      I should like to be considered for the post of Office Junior, advertised in the Evening Paper, dated 11th July, 1978.

      At the moment I am still at school, having completed my O-Level examinations in English Language, English Literature, General Science, Mathematics and Spanish. The
E results will not be published until August.

      My hobbies include tennis, squash and embroidery, and I am a member of the British Red Cross Society.

      The Headmaster of the school is aware of my application, and has stated that he will write a reference for me if that will be necessary. He has also told me that I may be released from lessons to attend an interview if you should wish.

                  F Yours faithfully,
                  G Jane Smith (Miss)

When you write a formal letter (sometimes known as a 'business letter') you must remember the following points:

A Your own address is written in full (and indented) in the top right-hand corner.

B The date is placed underneath your address. *Do* remember to include the date. Sometimes its omission can have serious consequences.

C On the left-hand side of the paper, some distance from the edge (about 25 mm), write the name and title and address of the person to whom the letter is being sent (i.e. the recipient). This address is *not* indented. The inclusion of this address is important. Failure to do so could delay your letter. Perhaps your teacher will explain why.

D Beneath this address you write the salutation (in this case 'Dear Sir' – as we do not know the name of the recipient).

E The body of the letter. This must not be 'chatty'. You should include all the necessary information and no more.

F At the end of this particular letter you must write 'Yours faithfully', with a capital 'Y' for 'Yours' and a small 'f' for 'faithfully'. If we had used the *name* of the recipient in the salutation (e.g. Dear Mr Smith) we should write 'Yours sincerely' at the end, with a capital 'Y' for 'Yours' and a small 's' for 'sincerely'.

G Finally you should write your signature – NOT *MISS SMITH* or *MR SMITH*.

WRITE THE FOLLOWING FORMAL LETTERS:

a A series of letters that might pass between the Manager of a large department store and you, and between the Manager and your parents – in which you and the prospects of a 'Saturday job' are discussed.

b A farmer has given some people permission to camp in his field which happens to be next to your garden. You object to their presence. Write letters to the farmer and to the campers, making your complaints known. Then write letters that might pass between: (*i*) the farmer and you, (*ii*) the campers and the farmer, (*iii*) the campers and you, and (*iv*) the farmer and the campers.

c Write a letter, on behalf of your class, asking the local police for information about cycle proficiency tests which some members of the class wish to take.

d Write a letter to the Director of a television programme, giving your opinion of it.

e Your Parent-Teacher Association has organised a money-raising social event. Write a letter, copies of which are to be sent to all parents, explaining what form the social will take, listing what is required and asking for volunteers to help.

f Your school is about to mount a safety campaign. Write to organisations like ROSPA, the fire service, and the British Red Cross Society, asking if they can provide you with advice and, perhaps, illustrations.

g Write a letter to your local Librarian, suggesting several titles that you would like to see on the shelves.

h Write to the Mayor of your town, asking him to visit your school in order to talk to the pupils about civic affairs.

i Several of you wish to go camping. Write to the Manager of a licensed site, asking for details of its organisation and making a provisional booking.

j Write to the proprietor of a riding school, asking for a copy of the prospectus.

k 'Wanted for September: Junior for large office. O-Levels in English Language and Mathematics required. Write for further details. Smith & Co., 14 Oak Square, Greenpark.'

Write a letter in answer to that advertisement, giving necessary information about your age, qualifications, experience and interests.

l Write a letter to a local landowner, asking permission to take a party hiking on his property.

m Write to the Headteacher of your school, inviting him/her to a buffet lunch to be held in the Home Economics Department.

n Write a letter to the Editor of a magazine, giving your opinion of an advertisement that has appeared in a recent issue.

o A group of young people wish to make themselves available for community service. Write a letter to the Editor of your local newspaper, asking him if he can advertise the fact in his editions.

p As Secretary of a school club (e.g. chess, cricket, netball) write to the Secretary of a similar club in a nearby school, suggesting that matches be organised.

q Having returned from a seaside holiday, you discover that you have left your camera behind in the holiday camp. Write a letter to the Manager of the establishment, describing the camera and asking him if he will kindly return it. You should offer to pay the postage, of course.

r Write to the Director of Parks, drawing his attention to the fact that swings in a children's play-ground are in a dangerous condition, probably as a result of vandalism.

s Write a letter of thanks to the Manager of a theatre who has shown you and a party round the building, introducing you to one or two well-known entertainers while doing so.

t Write to your local radio station, asking for a copy of a recipe that has been broadcast recently.

u Your local hospital has its own internal broadcasting system. Write to the Controller, asking that a certain record be played for a particular patient. Remember to give *all* necessary information.

v Your father's garage has finally collapsed. Write a letter to a local builder, asking him if he will call to give an estimate for the building of a new one.

Having written letters, we must send them to the recipients. Addresses on envelopes must be punctuated correctly, as in the following example:

> Mr J. P. Smith,
> 5 Wilson Avenue,
> SEATOWN,
> South Glamorgan.

Note
(*i*) The word 'Mr' requires no full-stop after it.

(*ii*) Initials *are* followed by full-stops.

(*iii*) A comma may or may not be placed after the number of the house. It is preferable to omit the comma, however, because a careless or untidy mark can, possibly, make the number look like 51 or 57, for example.

(*iv*) All words, except for 'Mr', 'Co.', and 'Ltd.', are written in full, e.g. Avenue, not Ave., Road, not Rd., Street, not St., etc.

(*v*) A comma is placed at the end of every line of the address until the last word is written (in this case 'Glamorgan') where a full-stop is necessary.

(*vi*) The name of the county may be abbreviated.

(*vii*) The name of the town is printed in capitals.

PUNCTUATE THE FOLLOWING ADDRESSES:

1 mrs g p james 12 olton road stetford notts
2 the manager fresh bakery east gardens flintlea yorks
3 rev c must the vicarage woolboard west midlands
4 mr and mrs g wells 15 peat grove lodestone derby
5 messrs c and p reed silk house mannington gwent

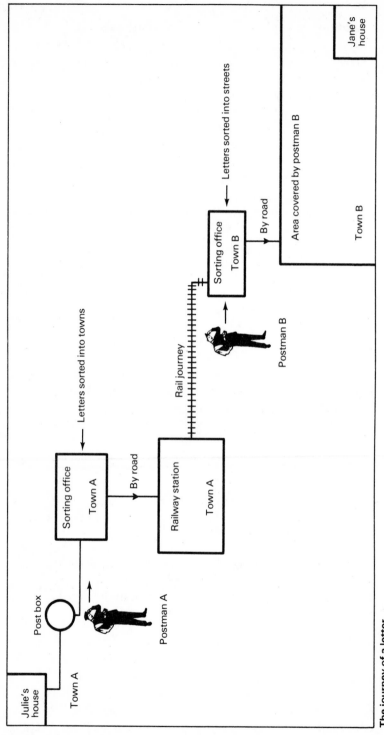

The journey of a letter

1 By referring to the diagram on page 22, explain how a letter written by Julie in Town A is delivered to Jane in Town B.

2 Describe the work done by Postman A so far as Julie's letter is concerned.

3 Describe the work done by Postman B so far as delivering the letter to Jane is concerned.

4 Write a letter to the Postmaster at Heath Road Post Office, Lington, explaining that you have been expecting a very important letter which has failed to arrive.

5 Describe a day in your working life, mentioning the pleasures and the difficulties experienced by (*i*) a country postman, and (*ii*) a city postman.

6 Explain how to address an envelope correctly.

7 Write the letter that might have been sent by Julie.

8 Write the answer that Jane might have sent.

Look at this photograph and then compose any piece of writing that it suggests to you:

Reports

Most people must have read a newspaper report at some time. Look at the following:

A director of a local manufacturing company was slightly injured last night when he lost control of his car at the traffic lights at Rowton Cross Roads. 'I braked,' said Mr D. Smith, 'but as I did so the steering-wheel was jerked out of my hands.' The car came to rest half-way through the window of a furniture shop. Mr Smith had been visiting friends and had decided to return home early as he was feeling unwell. 'It must have been something I ate,' he said. 'I certainly had nothing to drink.'

The car was extensively damaged, but Mr Smith said that he was grateful for his life.

A report – whatever type – is written in order to give some kind of information to the reader. Such information should be accurate and presented simply and clearly. In the report above you will notice that the 'victim' takes over at times from the reporter and some Direct Speech is used.

The *main* function of a newspaper is to tell its readers what is happening in the world, to give them the news in printed form:

Two children, John and Julie Lewis, were taken to Longpark General Hospital today after collapsing near Leafy Park. They had been playing on waste ground which is used for illegal dumping by several manufacturing companies. Exactly what caused the children's condition is not yet clear. Two lorry-drivers who visited the area earlier are being questioned by police.

Notice that only the essential facts of the case are given in the report. Other papers print the news, giving the essential facts, but telling it in what might be termed 'story form'. Such a report is more 'dramatic' than the one quoted above, making use of what is known as 'human interest'. Many people find this style of writing very suitable for reading on 'bus or train journeys as they commute to work:

Tonight eight-year old twins John and Julie Lewis are lying in Longpark General Hospital fighting for their lives. Local girl, Judith Williams, spotted the youngsters roaming about on a piece of waste ground next to the park where they were supposed to be playing. 'I told them not to play there,' said Miss Williams. 'I explained that people dumped dangerous chemicals there.'

The children went away, but after Miss Williams had left they apparently returned. They were discovered later, both unconscious. Their father is still unaware of the situation as he is on a long-distance trip to the West Country.

Newspaper space is very expensive. Consequently reports, while containing *all necessary information*, must be concise.

Before you write the reports suggested below it might be a good idea for you to read a large number of reports from different newspapers, noting their styles.

a A small boy has rescued a dog from a derelict house. Describe the rescue as it might be reported in a newspaper.

b Imagine that you are walking along a street one day when you see a car draw up at the curb outside an electrical shop. A man jumps out of the car, throws a brick through the shop window and snatches up some expensive-looking transistor radios. Then he returns to his car and drives away. The whole episode takes no more than a few seconds. Write a report, describing what you saw.

c Write a newspaper report, describing in detail a child who is missing from home.

d An 'unusual' person is living rough in the neighbourhood. Write a description of him as it might appear in a newspaper. Make your character interesting and unusual, but do not create a ridiculous monster. His clothes might be eccentric, but his physical appearance should not be horrific in any sense. In order to make him unusual you might concentrate on his strange habits, for example.

Write newspaper reports, two for each suggested headline, one as a straight-forward report of facts, the other from the 'human interest' point of view:

a Floods Devastate Holiday Village.

b Another M-Way Pile-up.

c Superstar Disappears.

d Farmers Wait! Where Is The Sun?

e Holiday-makers in Travel Chaos.

f Unknown Chosen to Represent Britain.

g Parachutist's Incredible Escape!

h Schoolgirls Set Up World Record.

i Oil-well in Back Garden!

j Cause for Whole Country to Celebrate.

Newspapers sometimes bring the plight of certain people to the notice of the public:

Tonight one man, seventy-two year old Mr John Jones, is making a final stand against a local authority. The house in which Mr Jones has lived for the past fifty-eight years is the last one standing in West Street in the town of Sourtham, the rest having been demolished to make way for a new super-store and multi-storey car-park. The Council has offered Mr Jones alternative accommodation, but he refuses to move.

'They want me to go to the other side of the town,' Mr Jones told our reporter when he interviewed him through barricaded windows today. 'I've got no friends there, and I'm too old to make new ones,' he added.

An official tonight said that Mr Jones will be out of his house tomorrow – 'one way or another'.

Write newspaper reports which are suggested by the following:

a Man Carries On His Lonely Vigil Outside Hospital.
b Woman Compelled To Resign.
c Farmer's Livelihood Threatened.
d Man Ordered To Destroy Illegal Garage.
e Corner Shop-keeper Forced Out of Business.

National newspapers are mainly concerned with national and international incidents and events. While local newspapers deal with wider issues, they concentrate on news that is peculiar to the areas that they serve.

Vandals who ran wild at Hill School found little reward for their actions. Between Saturday afternoon and early Monday morning intruders gained entry to the school by forcing a skylight above the science laboratory. There the thieves found only 40p – tea money collected from members of the staff.

Frustrated by their lack of financial success, the gang embarked on an orgy of destruction, breaking open cupboards, smashing bottles and jars and setting off fire-extinguishers. Powder paint was scattered over the floor of the art room, while exercise books were torn up and strewn about two of the classrooms.

Today the police were questioning a man and four youths.

(*i*) Have you any comments to make on the contents of that report?
(*ii*) Can you suggest why so many schools are attacked in this way?
(*iii*) How might such acts of vandalism be prevented?

Write reports for a local newspaper, dealing with the following topics:

a An accident.
b Plans for a new park.
c A shop fire.
d The annual carnival.
e A sports meeting.
f A charity event.
g Traffic chaos caused by road works.
h A visit by a celebrity.
i Damage at a children's playground.
j A reunion between friends or relatives who have been separated for many years.

Write reports suggested by the following headlines. Some of them would appear in national newspapers, while others would be found in local editions:

a Mystery Illness Reported in Four Cities.
b Britain Swelters in Heat-wave.
c Record Sum Raised At Easter Fayre.
d Jet Crashes On Circus! Miracle Escapes!
e Workmen Rescued From Collapsed Tunnel.
f Another Space Shot!
g Skating-rink Finally Re-opened.
h Boy Injured While On Holiday Ramble.
i Express Derailed.
j Super-star To Open Super-stores!
k 'Extinct' Volcano Erupts!
l Snow-storm Closes New Ring-road.
m Dogs Terrorise Estate.
n Fog Blankets Country.
o Oil Slick Threatens East Coast.
p Brigade Called To Hose Down Road.
q Teenager Crosses Channel Single-handed.
r Disused Station Turned Into Home.
s New Delays On M-Way.
t Family Off On Round-the-world Hike.

Compose any piece of writing suggested by this photograph:

Members of the public have the opportunity to express their opinions in print by writing 'Letters to the Editor':

Sir,

Recently I returned to this – my native city – after spending several years abroad, mainly on the Continent of Europe. I cannot adequately express the anger I felt as I walked in the well-planned and, to me, new, city centre. Litter was piled high in every conceivable corner. Discarded boxes, doubtless from a supermarket, had been thrown into the base of an ornamental fountain and left there. Greasy chip papers and wrappings blew about in all directions.

Have the people lost all pride in their city?

Yours,

E.P.S.

Dear Sir,

Your newspaper is always full of reports describing the loutish behaviour of teenagers. While what you print is true, surely you must know that the very large majority of young people are considerate and law-abiding. I noticed that you found no space to report on the two boys who, finding an old lady who had been attacked and robbed, saw her home safely, paying for a taxi out of the money they had earned from their early morning paper rounds.

Yours faithfully,

S. Walker (aged 15)

a Write a letter to the Editor, either supporting, or disagreeing with the author of the first letter quoted above.

b Write a letter from the Editor in answer to that written by S. Walker.

c Write letters to the Editor, suggested by the following:

(i) The lack of clubs and places of interest for young people in your area.

(ii) The poor display – in your opinion – presently on show at the local art gallery.

(iii) From a 'bus-driver, complaining about the behaviour of some members of the public while travelling on the 'buses.

(iv) From a housewife, complimenting the courtesy she has found while shopping in certain stores.

(v) From an old person, complaining about the untidy conditions of the city's parks.

(vi) Your purse (or wallet), having been handed to the police after you had lost it, prompts you to write to the Editor of the local paper, expressing your pleasure at discovering that there are still honest people in the world.

(vii) As the organiser of a charity flag-day you appeal for

volunteers by writing a letter to the Editor of your local newspaper. Give your potential helpers as much information as possible, but *concisely*.

(*viii*) From a farmer, urging city-dwellers who spend their week-ends in the countryside to obey the country code.

(*ix*) To the Editor, suggesting that his newspaper might include a page specially designed for young readers. You might suggest what items you would like to see included.

(*x*) A letter, giving your opinion of some piece of news recently reported in the paper.

A class project

One member of the class writes a 'Letter to the Editor' on any topic he or she chooses. The letter is then read aloud, or written on the black-board, and the other members of the class write their own answers to it.

Having finished, another individual writes another letter on a different topic and the others compose their answers.

Newpapers always excite curiosity. No one ever lays one down without a feeling of disappointment.

Charles Lamb

Have you any comment to make on that quotation?

Explain the following pairs of words which are frequently found in daily newspapers.

a	mini-market	b	Cabinet-minister
c	board-meeting	d	stereo-player
e	patio-door	f	central-heating
g	video-tape	h	comprehensive-insurance
i	electronic-device	j	freezer-centre
k	weather-forecast	l	transistor-radio
m	driving-licence	n	aircraft-carrier
o	best-seller	p	free-falling
q	computer-programmer	r	occupational hazard
s	roving reporter	t	pay-load
u	hire-purchase	v	national chain
w	rush-hour	x	corporal punishment
y	private tuition	z	self-righting

READ THE FOLLOWING REPORTS OF AN INTERVIEW:

Report (a)

Last week I talked to Mrs A. Taylor for our 'Meet the Ordinary People' Series. The following is a shortened version of the interview:

REPORTER You say your job is a little unusual, Mrs Taylor?

MRS TAYLOR I think it is. I'm a draughtswoman.

REPORTER Is that really unusual today?

MRS TAYLOR A little. In the office where I work there are eighteen draughtsmen – and me. That makes me a little 'unusual', don't you think?

REPORTER I suppose so. Why did you take up such work?

MRS TAYLOR I was a frustrated art student. At one time I imagined I was pretty good with a brush, until I left school and met real competition in the real world. There was no hope for me as an artist, so I settled for second-best.

REPORTER Surely you must long to do something creative?

MRS TAYLOR What I do *is* creative. It's *my* work. My designs often – and it's responsible work. My drawings have to be right – and a lot of people depend on me for their livelihoods, too. Besides, I can paint – my real love – for fun. Perhaps it's better like this. My real love is my hobby. If it became my work – well!

REPORTER In these days of equality do you find that you are treated the same as the men in your office?

MRS TAYLOR Exactly! I'm reprimanded when necessary, the same as the men are. I suppose the boss *does* treat me a little more gently sometimes.

REPORTER What about promotion?

MRS TAYLOR What *about* promotion? There's little chance in my firm. There's just the boss and us.

REPORTER And what exactly do you draw?

MRS TAYLOR Parts of machines. Parts of engines. It varies.

REPORTER So the work doesn't get boring?

MRS TAYLOR Occasionally. I should think all work gets boring at times. If I'm to believe my friends, that is . . .

You will have noticed in that extract that the interviewee (i.e. the person being interviewed) did more talking than did the Reporter. That is as an interview should be. After all, the reader is not particularly interested in the Reporter.

Report (b)

Now read the same interview again:

Last week I talked to Mrs A. Taylor for our 'Meet the Ordinary People' Series. I found the lady in the canteen next to the drawing-office where she has worked for six years. She thought that her work as a draughtswoman was a little unusual. She said, 'In the office where I work there are eighteen draughtsmen and me.'

When I asked Mrs Taylor why she took up that particular line of work she smiled, a little sadly, I thought. 'I was a frustrated art student,' she confessed. 'At one time I imagined I was pretty good with a brush, until I left school and met real competition in the real world.' It was then that she decided that there was no hope of success for her as an artist, so she chose 'second-best'.

Even so, Mrs Taylor is not really 'frustrated' in her daily work. She believes that what she is doing is, in fact, creative, despite the doubts I cast. She is also aware of the responsibility of her task. 'My drawings have to be right – and a lot of people depend on them for their livelihoods,' she told me. She went on to explain that she could still paint – as a hobby, and as her real love is painting her hobby is worthwhile.

I returned to my first question, or an offshoot of that question, about her being 'unusual'. 'What about equality?' I asked. Was she treated the same as the men?

Her answer was definite. 'Exactly!' Reprimands fall on her just as they do on the men, but she did admit that the 'boss' was a little gentle with her at times.

'And what about promotion?'

'There's little chance in my firm,' she said, but not at all bitterly. 'There's just the boss and us,' she added.

I wondered just what it was that Mrs Taylor actually drew in her office.

'Parts of machines. Parts of engines. It varies,' she answered. And was she ever bored?

'Occasionally. I should think all work gets boring at times. If I am to believe my friends. . . .'

In the second version of the report some of the same words are used as we read in the first, but they have been 'connected' by the Reporter's words.

Write reports, two for each as above, based on these suggestions:
a An interview with a well-known personality.
b An interview with your teacher or Headteacher. This may be real or imaginary.
c An interview with someone who has just made a record balloon flight.
d An interview with an old pupil who has come back to visit the school.
e Interviews with the following: a dentist; a factory worker; a street-corner newspaper seller.

Punctuation

> Manchester
> London
> The North
> The South

The man looking at the sign might well be confused! While the sign is large enough and clearly printed – *no directions* are given.

Many signs that we see and use daily are intended for our *guidance*.

In a similar way punctuation is really intended to guide the reader, to help him make sense of the words in front of him. When we are speaking we are not aware of punctuation because we use pauses, and raise and lower the pitch of our voices in order to make sense to our listeners. When we write we have to indicate these pauses and changes of pitch by employing signs such as full-stops, commas, apostrophes, question-marks and quotation-marks. There are other signs, of course, but those mentioned are the ones most commonly mis-used, or omitted altogether.

Theoretically we should all be able to use punctuation easily and correctly, having been able to do so from a very early age. In practice this is not true, as teachers of English and Examiners in English from all over the country will testify.

Most boys and girls, if asked, would say that a sentence is a group of words that make complete sense, but when they *write* they so often fail to do what they say, writing sentences which are, in fact, *not* sentences. They will also *say* that all sentences should begin with capital letters and end with full-stops!

Look at the following and decide which are sentences and which are not, giving your reason for your decision in each case:

a The gate was left open.
b Jack arrived at midnight.
c At the side of the pool.
d Anne completed her homework by eight o'clock.
e When the sun shone.

f The little old man.

g It is almost time to go home.

h The new book.

i Last Wednesday the two boys.

j The aeroplanes crashed on take-off.

How many did you get right?

Types of sentences

Here, again, most pupils know that there are several types of sentences.

1 *A statement sentence* is one in which something is stated.

e.g. The bird flew away.

2 *A question sentence* is one in which something is asked – and it *must* end with a question-mark.

e.g. What is the time, please?

3 In a *command sentence* some order is given.

e.g. Finish your work quickly.

4 An *exclamation sentence* is one which is spoken in an excited manner. It ends with an exclamation-mark.

e.g. No! It can't be!

Of the four, the first two seem to give the most trouble to pupils. In the second they frequently omit the question-mark. Statement sentences are, undoubtedly, the most abused.

A simple statement sentence contains *one statement*.

e.g. The sun shone.

Problems arise when pupils write two (or more) statements and *join them with a comma*.

i.e. The sun shone, the sky was blue.

In order to make a single sentence into a double sentence (i.e. making TWO statements in ONE sentence) a joining word – and NOT a comma – must be used.

e.g. The sun shone *and* the sky was blue.

Usually no punctuation is necessary when using such joining words as 'and' or 'or'. A comma is required when using 'yet' or 'but' because these words introduce contrast into the sentence.

e.g. The sun shone, but the wind was cold.

Join the following simple sentences so that they become double sentences. There *are* other joining words besides 'and', 'but', 'or' and 'yet'.

a Jack was early. Mary arrived late.

b The dog barked loudly. It growled fiercely.

c The old man shivered. He stood at the 'bus-stop.

d I like apples. I dislike plums.

e We saw ships on the sea. We saw aeroplanes in the sky.

f The girls giggled. The boys were annoyed.

g We caught the first 'bus to town. We arrived late.

h June won the race. She injured her foot.

i He saw the accident. He told no one about it.

j The policeman chased the man. He caught him at the end of the road.

Punctuate this passage, putting in all necessary full-stops, commas and capital letters:

the morning sky was clear and blue when the boys set off it was half an hour later when the first clouds appeared they were black and heavy the boys shivered as the wind began to blow fiercely then the rain fell for a while they walked on but soon they were forced to take shelter in an old barn there they remained for more than half an hour finally they could stay no longer

Compose any piece of writing that this photograph suggests:

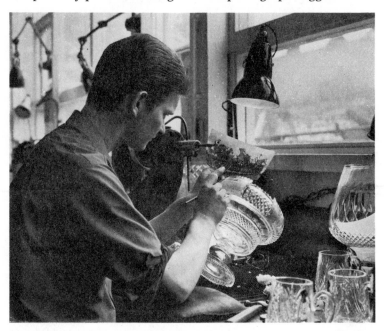

Projects

There are various ways of producing 'projects'. Those suggested here are meant to be class efforts, but you may make them individual offerings, of course.

First of all the topics should be fully discussed and reference books consulted. If 'experts' can be contacted and their first-hand experience utilised, so much the better. All important information should be noted – ready for the written work – which might take various forms such as informal letters, formal letters, interviews, descriptions, reports and diaries. The written work might be supplemented by sketches, drawings, plans, graphs, photographs, posters, pictures, models and tape-recordings.

A project that is well-planned, well-produced and well-presented can be a very satisfactory piece of work, besides being useful, and informative.

a A 'ghost town'

In some parts of the world it is possible to discover towns and villages which are quite deserted, the people having left for some reason. Such places are often known as 'ghost towns'. Imagine that you have been 'given' one of these places and it is up to you to make it live again. That means that you have to fill it with people – e.g. shop-keepers, a doctor, at least one clergyman, a teacher, an architect, health workers, plumbers, electricians, builders, members of the Council, a Mayor, policemen, 'bus-drivers and so on.

b The community and the school

Many schools today are known as 'Community Schools' or 'Community Colleges'. They are meant to be social centres for the communities which surround them. The equipment and facilities of such places are used in the evenings and at weekends by members of that community. Who *are* the members of the community – your community? When you have discovered who these people are you might be able to interview them. If you can, write up the interviews and present them in a folder. If you cannot interview them, then use your imaginations.

c A club

Many people are involved in the building and setting up of a new club: architects, bankers, bricklayers, carpenters, electricians, caterers, furnishers, members of the club management and so on. Imagine that the members of your form propose setting up a new club. Make a list of the people who would be concerned in its building and establishment and then write a series of letters to and from the various people. You might include reports of some interviews.

d A common article – e.g. a cardigan or a crash-helmet.

Trace the people who might be concerned in the production of the article. Then write a series of interviews with these people in which you discuss their work, home life, leisure and so on.

e A survey (This may be real or imaginary.)

Take a group of people (e.g. teenagers, the twenty to thirty year age group, old-aged pensioners) and conduct a survey to investigate, for example, the ways in which they spend their leisure-time, or their opinions on any particular topics. Write the completed project in the form of letters, interviews, and reports.

Stories

Write stories suggested by the following, concentrating on building up vivid pictures of the characters:

a The nightwatchman.
b A village policeman.
c The Light-house.
d An unwelcome visitor.
e The day we explored the old house.
f A visit to the circus.
g The wax-works.
j A wonderful party.
i Castaway on a desert island.
j First on Mars.

Diaries

Most of us have been given diaries at some time, and most of us have been determined to write in them every day. It is probably true to say that after a few days, certainly after several weeks, we have failed in our resolutions for one reason or another.

Fortunately for us there have been people in the past who made entries in their diaries every day – and we still have them. It is from such books that we have learned a considerable amount of the history of our country – from 'first-hand' we might say.

Read the following extract taken from a diary. If it were true – can you say to what sort of person it belonged?

SUNDAY	Didn't attend church this morning. Headache. Better by tea-time. Went to Evensong. Visiting preacher. His sermon long and boring.
MONDAY	Went to shop early. Sales started today. Crowds very indisciplined. Some damage done to several garments. No more Sales till June. Very grateful.
TUESDAY	Uneventful day. Poor turn-out of choristers at evening practice. Tonight – new Easter Anthem.
WEDNESDAY	Half-closing. Afternoon – played squash with Ted.
THURSDAY	Very busy at shop. Blouse damaged by discarded cigarette-end. A filthy and dangerous habit! Jean not at work. These youngsters have

	no stamina. Any excuse to take day off. The younger generation annoy me. I often wonder if *anyone* can understand them – especially themselves. Checked motor on organ-blower. Seems to be something wrong with it. Must be repaired for special service Sunday.
FRIDAY	Quiet day. Business steady. Cinema with Mary. Poor film.
SATURDAY	Left Jean in charge of shop during afternoon while I visited church with organ specialist. Motor can't be fixed in time for tomorrow. Jean did well at shop. Sorry I thought badly of her on Thursday.

We learn several things about the writer from that extract. He is a church organist. He owns a shop. (How do we know that he is not an assistant?) He is a non-smoker, and he is probably middle-aged.

Write diaries for one or two weeks for each of the following, trying to reveal something of the characters of the writers:

a Oliver Twist. You should read the book of that title before attempting this.

b The Mayor of your town. If it is not possible to discover how the Mayor spends his time officially you might read the local newspaper for a week or two, noting the various duties performed and the functions attended by him/her. 'Unofficial' entries for the diary might be imagined.

c A tramp. No help offered here. See what your imaginations can do.

d A castaway on a desert island. You might mention what he/she eats, sees, hears, and how he/she occupies himself/herself.

e Julius Caesar – or any famous person in history about whom you have learned. Try to mention items that were peculiar or special to the person named. For example, we can all have headaches, go to parties, and miss the 'bus, but we are not Roman Emperors!

f A teacher. Perhaps you might include observations on some of your pupils – on *you*, for example.

g A disc-jockey. He does not play records *all* the time, remember.

h A pupil at a boarding-school a hundred years or more ago. Again remember what you have learned in your lessons. You might also read such books as 'David Copperfield', 'Jane Eyre', 'Tom Brown's Schooldays', or 'Nicholas Nickleby'.

i A long-distance lorry-driver. If you know a real driver he might help you.

j A coal-miner. If you do not know a real miner there are many books on the subject and, no doubt, you have had lessons on it.

The page from a diary shown below contains only the briefest of information. Imagine that it is yours, and write a full account of your week's activities as suggested by the entries:

SUNDAY	Morning – Rusty to training school. Afternoon – park with others.
MONDAY	Practice after school.
TUESDAY	Careers interview 11 a.m. Parents invited.
WEDNESDAY	Local history lesson in shopping centre.
THURSDAY	Detention. Whole class. 4–5 p.m.
FRIDAY	Club night.
SATURDAY	Morning – town. Afternoon – match. Evening – disco.

Discussions

a The more I see of men, the more I admire dogs.

Attributed to **Mme de Sevigné**

Can you suggest any reasons why anyone should make such a statement?

b Other people are quite dreadful. The only possible society is oneself.

From *An Ideal Husband* by **Oscar Wilde**

Do other people ever appear 'dreadful' to you?

c Thou shalt love thy neighbour as thyself.

St. Matthew, 19:19

How far is it possible to do this?

Compose any pieces of writing suggested by these quotations:

a Dear God! the very houses seem asleep.

From *Upon Westminster Bridge* by **W. Wordsworth**

b When blood is nipped, and ways be foul
  Then nightly sings the staring owl.

William Shakespeare

c Then a mile of warm scented beach;
  Three fields to cross till a farm appears;
  A tap at the pane . . .

Robert Browning

d Down dropt the breeze, the sails dropt down,
  'Twas sad as sad could be;
  And we did speak only to break
  The silence of the sea.

From *The Rime of the Ancient Mariner* by **S. T. Coleridge**

e Youth's the season made for joys.

John Gay

3 PLACES

So far we have concentrated on describing people and creating characters, but much of our writing, especially stories, requires much more. We have to put our characters in some *place*, for example. Think of television stories for a moment. They all happen *somewhere*. If they did not then the players would perform in an empty room. Would *you* find that interesting?

Every year many people spend a considerable amount of time poring over brightly-coloured brochures, trying to choose a resort at which to spend their holidays. 'What sort of place is it?' they usually ask.

Having decided where to go, they frequently read as much information about it as possible so that when they actually go on the holiday they can really appreciate the *place*.

Look at this advertisement:

For the best holiday of your life – why not come and stay with us at the Fab Hotel? We are *near the sea* and there are many *fine views* to be enjoyed.

The excellence of our food is *well-known* and *many of the bedrooms* are superbly luxurious. Enjoy colour television in your own room after an enjoyable day out. You will find a *wealth of gentle walks* to help you encourage that healthy appetite.

What about children? They are welcome, of course, and, *within easy travelling distance*, you will discover one of the best fun-fairs in the country, with exciting rides for all the family.

Would you like to spend a holiday at that hotel? It sounds friendly and inviting, but what does it *really* say? Or *not* say?

'*Near the sea*' How near? Across the road? Within walking distance? Ten minutes could be 'near' if you had a fast car.

'*many of the bedrooms are superbly luxurious*.' What about the other bed-rooms? It does not state that *all* rooms are luxurious.

'*fine views*.' From where? The hotel? A beauty-spot miles away? And what about the quality of the food being '*well-known*'? By whom? The hotel chef and cooks? The hotel staff?

'*a wealth of gentle walks*.' This sounds fine for people who want a restful holiday, but what about those who enjoy something more vigorous?

'*within easy travelling distance*.' Travelling how? Walking? Driving? By train? By jet aeroplane?

Look at this advertisement. Read it and compare it with the first one:

Do you want the perfect holiday? Then come to SANDSEA! Six miles of glorious sand! Safe bathing! A kind climate all the year round. Family chalets to take from four to ten people. Every chalet comfortably furnished, each with own bath, shower and television set.

What about entertainment?

At SANDSEA we have plenty for everyone – and everything is FREE. Walks in beautiful countryside – boating-pools – golf – fishing – shooting – pony-trekking – tennis – heated swimming-pools – bingo – fun-fair . . . and all within a radius of two miles.

Daily excursions to famous beauty-spots and places of interest. . . .

It is possible that one day you will wish to buy a house – and it will be very costly, probably the most expensive item you will ever purchase. That being so, you will wish to examine the property to be sure that you are getting value for your money. One of the first stages in the process is 'looking at the market'. You will read many advertisements like that below – advertisements describing *places*.

FOR SALE

PROPERTY: A delightful modern detached house known as 1 The Meads, Towton.

LOCATION: Popular position overlooking Green Park. Close to traffic-free shopping precinct, schools and public transport.

DETAILS: Detached residence in quiet street.
Residential area.
Freehold.
Rateable Value:

GROUND FLOOR:
Large entrance-hall with wall-fixed gas heater.
Through Lounge/Dining area (25' × 12')
Area may be separated by folding doors.
Fitted book-shelves; gas fire. Patio double-glazed door leading to rear garden.

KITCHEN
12' × 6' 6". Half-tiled walls. Stainless steel sink. Single draining-board. Wall-fitted cupboard. Breakfast bar. Four electric points.

UPSTAIRS:
Bedroom 1: 12' × 10'

Bedroom 2: 11' × 8'
Bedroom 3: 8' × 7'6". Airing-cupboard.
BATHROOM:
Panelled bath. Pale blue suite. Low-level toilet.
Medicine cabinet. Water heated by immersion
heater.
OUTSIDE:
Small front garden. Long well-cultivated rear
garden. Brick garage for small car. Direct car access
at side of house.
May be viewed by appointment.
PRICE: ....

Having read the advertisement, the next step is to visit the
actual house. Sometimes it is interesting to see how different from
the written description the place really is.

You should also know exactly what is meant by such terms as
'Freehold' and 'Rateable Value'.

Imagine that you are an estate agent who has to put up *your*
house for sale. Write a description as it might appear in an
advertisement such as that above.

Such descriptions, however, would hardly find a place in
literature unless, of course, the story calls for a house to be sold.
Descriptions in literature are intended to engage our interest, to
please, to frighten, to thrill, to move the story on, to create a
certain atmosphere and so on.

What 'atmosphere' is created in this passage?

The garden was a wide enclosure, surrounded with walls so high as to
exclude every glimpse of prospect; a covered veranda ran down one
side, and broad walks bordered a middle space divided into scores of
little beds; these beds were assigned as gardens for the pupils to
cultivate, and each bed had an owner. When full of flowers they would
doubtless look pretty, but now, at the latter end of January, all was
wintry blight and brown decay. I shuddered as I stood and looked
round me: it was an inclement day for outdoor exercise – not positively
rainy, but darkened by a drizzling yellow fog; all underfoot was still
soaking wet with the floods of yesterday. The stronger among the girls
ran about and engaged in active games, but sundry pale and thin ones
herded together for shelter and warmth in the veranda; and amongst
these, as the dense mist penetrated to their shivering frames, I heard
frequently the sound of a hollow cough.

From *Jane Eyre* by **Charlotte Brontë**

a Write a diary for one week as it might have been written by one
of the girls at this school.

43

b Are you ever bored with school? Why? What problems might face your teachers?

c What is your attitude to school? Have you anything to say about such an attitude?

d How would you improve school, given the opportunity to do so?

e Do places affect you? Describe a particular place that depresses you.

f People are frequently encouraged (or 'driven') by the places in which they live (their environments) to do something to benefit mankind. For example – people who were brought up in conditions of extreme poverty have struggled to improve conditions so that others will not have to suffer in the same way. Some fine doctors and scientists who have fought to conquer diseases might well have seen members of their own families ravaged by those very diseases.

Do you know, or have you read of, someone who, because of his/her environment, 'did something for mankind'? Write a brief biography of him/her.

g You live in a 'Welfare State'. Do you know what that means? When you have found out, write a description of the benefits brought to our lives by such a state.

Having done so, see what you can discover about the conditions of life for ordinary people two hundred years ago. Then write an account and compare it with your first piece of writing in (g). Which century appeals more to you? Why?

h Using information learned in your History lessons, or from your own reading, describe a work-house of the Nineteenth Century. There might even be the remains of such a place near your home.

Here is a description of another place:

The Kitchen

The kitchen, worn by our boots and lives, was scruffy, warm and low, whose fuss of furniture seemed never the same but was shuffled around each day. A black grate crackled with coal and beech-twigs; towels toasted on the guard; the mantel was littered with fine old china, horse brasses, and freak potatoes. On the floor were strips of muddy matting, the windows were choked with plants, the walls supported stopped clocks and calendars, and smoky fungus ran over the ceiling. There were also six tables of different sizes, some armchairs gapingly stuffed, boxes, stools, and unravelling baskets, books and papers on every chair, a sofa for cats, a harmonium for coats, and a piano for dust and photographs. These were the shapes of our kitchen landscape, the rocks of our submarine life, each object worn smooth by our constant nuzzling, or encrusted by lively barnacles, relics of birthdays and dead relations, wrecks of furniture long since floundered, all silted deep by Mother's newspapers which the years piled round on the floor.

From *Cider With Rosie* by **Laurie Lee**

a This kitchen does not appear to have been particularly tidy, yet it gives one the impression that it was a happy place. Do you agree? If you do, can you say what it is that creates such an impression?

b Do you feel that the people who used this kitchen were happy? Why do you think so? Does this suggest that there is something in our lives which is much more important than any place? What is that 'something'?

'Compass Rose.'

In his book, *The Cruel Sea*, Nicholas Monsarrat describes conditions aboard the tiny ship, the corvette named *Compass Rose*.

Aboard Compass Rose, conditions were indescribable. She rolled furiously, with a tireless malice allowing no rest for anyone. Cooking was impossible, even had they not exhausted their fresh meat and vegetables many days previously: the staple diet was tea and corned beef, at breakfast, lunch, and dinner, for nearly a fortnight on end. Everything was wet through: some water had come down a ventilator and flooded the wardroom; Forward the mess-decks were a crowded hell of saturated clothes, spare gear washing about round their feet, food overturned – and all the time the noise, the groaning slamming violence of a small ship fighting a monstrous sea. There seemed no end to it. Compass Rose, caught in a storm which could take hold of her bodily and shake her till the very rivets loosened: a storm which raged and screamed at her and never blew itself out until they were in the shelter of the land again: Compass Rose adrift on this malignant ocean, seemed doomed to ride it forever.

From *The Cruel Sea* by **Nicholas Monsarrat**

a During wartime all sorts of people have to tolerate conditions which are often absolutely appalling. Have you ever been in a particularly uncomfortable situation? Can you describe how you felt at the time?

b Write a description of a pleasure cruise during a seaside holiday.

THE DESERTED VILLAGE

> Sweet was the sound when oft at evening's close,
> Up yonder hill the village murmur rose;
> There as I past with careless steps and slow,
> The mingling notes came softened from below;

The swain responsive as the milk-maid sung,
The sober herd that lowed to meet their young;
The noisy geese that gabbled o'er the pool,
The playful children just let loose from school;
The watch-dog's voice that bayed the whispering wind,
And the loud laugh that spoke the vacant mind,
These all in soft confusion sought the shade,
And filled each pause the nightingale had made.
But now the sounds of population fail,
No cheerful murmurs fluctuate in the gale,
No busy steps the grass-green foot-way tread,
But all the bloomy flush of life is fled.
All but yon widowed, solitary thing
That feebly bends beside the plashy spring;
She, wretched matron, forced, in age, for bread,
To strip the brooks with mantling cresses spread,
To pick her wintry faggots from the thorn,
To seek her nightly shed, and weep till morn;
She only left of all the harmless train,
The sad historian of the pensive plain.

by **Oliver Goldsmith**

Here the poet has described a place – a village – as it is now and as
he remembered it in earlier years. It is now deserted, but there
was a time when it was bustling with life. The overall picture
painted is one of peace. You will have noticed that he has used at
least two of his *senses*. He *heard* the 'village murmur', the cows
that 'lowed to meet their young', the geese, the voices of the
children, the baying of the dog, the 'whispering wind'.

He saw the 'wretched matron' who had to 'strip the brook' and
'pick her wintry faggots'.

Remembering your *senses*, write the following:

a A paragraph describing a place and aiming to create an
   atmosphere of peace. Choose your place carefully. For example,
   a supermarket on a Saturday, or the first day of the Sales would
   hardly be good choices to help you paint a quiet scene. On the
   other hand, you could think of a summer evening at a remote
   lakeside, or a seaside village in the moonlight.

b A paragraph in which you create a picture of a busy
   marketplace, suggesting an atmosphere of bustle. Remember
   that you can *see* things, *hear* sounds. There will be various
   smells such as fruit, vegetables, leather, hot-dogs, fish. You
   might even *taste* things.

c It is not too difficult in towns and cities to find a derelict building. If you know of such a place see how well you can describe it. If you live in the country it will not be so easy to find such a subject about which to write, but you *do* have your imagination.

d Write a vivid description, not forgetting *sounds* as well as *sights*, of the countryside around you at particular times of the year, e.g. after a winter snow-fall, during a storm, at harvest time.

e Write a description of a very old building or an unusual building.

f Write a description of a junk-shop and of some of the items there. You can make your task a little easier if you choose to write about items worthy of description.

g Take three or four 'strange' or 'unusual' items that might be found in the junk-shop in 'f' and write descriptions of each. Try to invent good reasons why the owners parted with them.

h The modern articles which you use and see all about you will, one day, be 'old-fashioned'. Describe two or three of your own possessions that might be considered as old-fashioned in years to come. Having done so, try to imagine and describe what you think might replace them.

i Look at the photograph and then compose any piece of writing that it suggests to you:

j Imagine that you and your class have spent a day at Manor House Park shown in the sketch-map on p. 48.

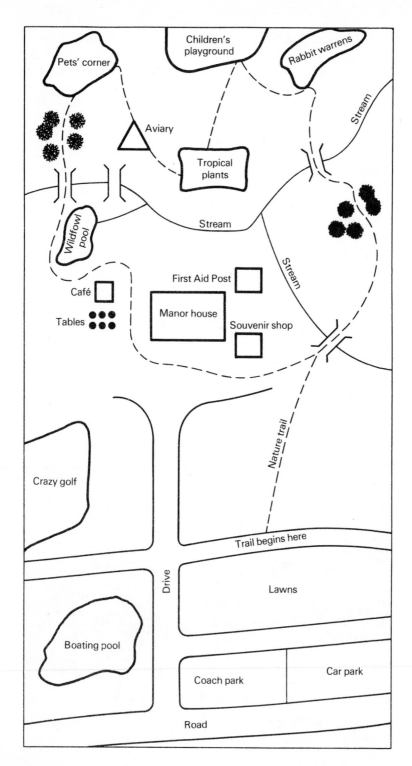

(i) Describe the coach journey to the Park.

(ii) Describe what you saw when you walked along the nature trail, which is indicated by the broken line.

(iii) Having been on a conducted tour with your teacher, you were allowed to spend two hours in the grounds to go where you pleased. Explain how you spent your time.

(iv) During the visit you suffered a minor accident. Explain how it happened, and describe the treatment you received.

(v) Describe the souvenirs you bought for the various members of your family, saying why you chose the particular items.

(vi) Write your opinion of school visits as if you were: the owner of the Manor House; a coach-driver responsible for taking the parties to the Park; the Cafe Manager; the first-aid officer on duty; the groundsman; the person in charge of Pets' Corner; the car-park attendant.

(vii) Write out a list of rules that might be necessary for the safe and orderly running of such a day-trip. Give reasons for each regulation.

k Write a description of a holiday resort that you like, giving your reasons.

l Now describe a holiday resort that you dislike, also giving reasons.

Using Words

There is no adequate substitute for good reading if you wish to increase your vocabulary. When you come across a new word discover its meaning by using a good dictionary. Having done so, practise using the word, correctly, in your own writing until it becomes part of your daily language.

In order to increase your vocabulary further, consult a thesaurus to discover if the new word has other words similar in meaning, or opposite in meaning.

A thesaurus is indispensable to the writer. It is a book containing thousands of words and their synonyms (i.e. words similar in meaning).

Take the word 'ghost', for example. In a thesaurus we might find an entry something like this:

GHOST: Nouns: spirit; poltergeist; spectre; shade; phantom; apparition; wraith.

Adjectives: spiritualistic; spectral; ghostly; supernatural; macabre; eerie.

Or the word 'smell':

SMELL: *Nouns:* odour; aroma; perfume; scent; stink; bouquet;
fumes; reek.

Adjectives: aromatic; odorous; perfumed; scented;
stinking; reeking.

Vocabulary practice

1 Write synonyms (i.e. words similar in meaning) for the
following words:

a	apparel	b	ascertain
c	bargain	d	obstacle
e	principal	f	ultimate
g	onlooker	h	list
i	prominent	j	pray

2 Explain the difference between the following pairs of words:

a	band, orchestra	b	cinema, theatre
c	physician, surgeon	d	famous, well-known
e	picture, photograph	f	gate, door
g	stool, chair	h	newspaper, magazine
i	balcony, veranda	j	cushion, pillow
k	convector, radiator	l	brief, concise
m	lonely, solitary	n	house, home

3 Write antonyms (i.e. words opposite in meaning) to the
following:

a	disclose	b	frivolous
c	irritating	d	rare
e	scarce	f	vacant
g	prohibit	h	wise
i	absence	j	industrious

4 Write antonyms for the following by adding a prefix (i.e. a
letter or letters) to the beginning of each word:
e.g. legible – *il*legible.

a	responsible	b	human
c	noble	d	interesting
e	literate	f	sensible
g	significant	h	religious
i	correct	j	considerate

Many English words have more than one meaning:
e.g. ape – an animal

ape – to copy
crow – a bird
crow – to boast

Write sentences, two for each, showing that these words may be used with more than one meaning:

a tender   b exhaust   c grave   d fire   e shed
f dog   g book   h court   i show   j engineer

It is possible to give words two meanings by varying the accent or emphasis:

e.g. converse – to speak together
     *con*verse – opposite
     refuse – not to accept
     *ref*use – rubbish or waste

Write sentences, two for each word, to show that varying the accent alters the meanings of these words:

a concert   b discount   c invalid   d import   e contract
f convict   g conduct   h frequent i object   j envelope

Write ONE word for each of the following groups of words. The initial letter is given as a clue:

1 an outline seen against a background of a different colour. (S)
2 possessed of a friendly nature. (A)
3 one who attacks another. (A)
4 a liquid that may be drunk. (B)
5 a person who eats no meat. (V)
6 a person who has reached the age of one hundred years. (C)
7 the practice of collecting stamps. (P)
8 a creature which has four legs. (Q)
9 to make up for a loss sustained. (R)
10 one who supervises candidates in an examination. (I)
11 the partition between the chest and the abdomen. (D)
12 one who looks on the brighter side of life. (O)
13 having to do with horsemanship. (E)
14 something that is not extinct. (E)
15 a person who presides over a court of law. (M)
16 to think deeply. (M)
17 a sad longing for days that have gone. (N)
18 something that has gone out of use. (O)
19 having the quality of photographing well. (P)
20 a mischievous spirit which is said to disarrange furniture. (P)
21 permitting light, but not vision, to pass through. (T)
22 an action performed on impulse. (S)

23 a person who escorts patrons to their seats in a cinema. (U)
24 unable to make a decision. (V)
25 the centre of a whirlpool. (V)
26 the practice of spying. (E)
27 forced isolation to prevent contraction, or spreading, of disease. (Q)
28 one capable of speaking and writing several languages. (L)
29 one interested in the study of birds. (O)
30 something to counteract a poison. (A)

Read the following passage, noting that the writer has used a varying vocabulary, employing synonyms such as: darkness-blackness; scream-cry; mine-shaft-cavern; ghost-spirit-spectre.

How long Billy had been unconscious he had no idea, for when he awoke he was in total darkness, a darkness he had never known before. Of course! The roof of the mine-shaft had collapsed, had imprisoned him deep in the earth. Whether it was night or day outside he had no way of telling.

For a moment he lay in the blackness of the cavern, hardly realising the horror of his situation. Since he could remember he had been appalled by the thought of being trapped in enclosed spaces. When the truth made itself known to him his terror was boundless. He lay paralysed.

'I'm buried,' he murmured. 'I'm buried alive.' He screamed, but the earth and rubble that choked the tunnel muffled his cry. 'No one will hear,' he sobbed. 'No one.'

Again he slept. And he dreamed – that he was in a strange place. 'The haunted house,' someone whispered. 'You're in the haunted house, Billy.'

'Haunted!' He laughed aloud – in the dream. 'Nothing's haunted.' He had barely finished saying the word when he heard a clanking noise. Chains! Ghosts dragged chains, didn't they?

Suddenly he was no longer alone. A strange visitor stood before him. 'Who are you?' gasped Billy.

'A ghost!'

Billy looked at the spectre.

'A real ghost?'

The spirit nodded its head. 'Real! I'm haunting you!'

Billy shuddered. Why had he always laughed when others talked about phantoms? Here he was – looking at a real one.

Again he awoke, shivering from the dream. . . .

Letters

Remembering what you have already learned, write the following letters:

a To a friend, describing the school you attend. You might take a paragraph to describe the general appearance of the building, a paragraph for the inside and a paragraph to tell your friend about anything interesting that you do – such as unusual lessons or using special equipment. Try to avoid developing the letter into a series of complaints.

b Imagine that you have a pen-friend who lives a considerable distance away, maybe abroad. Write a letter in which you describe your town or village. Try to mention some really interesting features.

c Write to your parents, describing the holiday resort at which you are staying. Your parents will probably be a little worried about your being away, so try to reassure them.

d Imagine that you have left home in order to work in another town. Write to your parents, describing the job, the place of employment and your 'digs'.

e Having moved to a new house, write to your old neighbours and tell them all about it.

f Describe the places that you like and those you dislike in the area in which you live. You might also include your reasons.

g Write to a friend, making the main item in the letter a description of a place of interest that you have visited.

h Imagine that you are convalescing after an illness and you are confined to your bedroom. Write a letter to a friend, describing your sick-room and the view from it. You will probably mention your feelings, but do not dwell on them. In other words, do not make your letter a means of indulging in self-pity. Indeed, it would be far better to aim at writing a cheerful letter.

Punctuation

School pupils are either generous with their commas, sprinkling them indiscriminately throughout their work, or positively miserly, failing to include them at all. Commas, like full-stops, are necessary signs to help the reader.

These particular punctuation marks are required in several situations, but the three that follow here are those that appear to be constantly misunderstood.

1 Commas are used to separate items in a list. More often than not the comma is omitted before the 'and' that introduces the final item.

e.g. We bought nails, screws, a hammer and a saw.
During the holidays John visited France, Belgium, Holland and Germany.

2 Commas are used to isolate phrases that are not essential to the main sentence and which could be omitted without altering the sense of the sentence.

e.g. John, who can speak several languages, hopes to start work next week.

NOTE: If we take out the words inside the commas the main sentence remains unchanged –

John hopes to start work next week.

The words 'who can speak several languages' simply add a little extra interest to the sentence.

3 Commas are necessary when writing speech to separate the words actually spoken from the rest of the sentence.

e.g. John said, 'I hope to go to town tomorrow.'

'What is the time?' asked Linda.

Writing Direct Speech presents many pupils with problems. Here, again, when asked to punctuate sentences containing speech, most of them can cope adequately. Yet a large number of them, when writing speech in an essay, seem to forget all they have ever been taught about punctuation. This suggests that many pupils simply do not *think before they write*.

Look at the following:

Mary   John

Comics, magazines, newspapers and some books, especially annuals, use characters whose speech is printed in balloons as you see in the example above. If we tried to write *all* the conversation in a book in the same manner we should have to produce a very thick volume because so much space would be required. Instead we employ a much more economical method with the use of quotation, or speech, marks.

e.g. Mary said, 'Bill crashed into a wall on his motor-cycle last night.'

'We all said he'd do that one day,' said John.

You should notice that instead of drawing a picture of Mary her name only has been written. The words which she *actually* spoke and which were inside the balloon are now *inside the speech marks*. In order that the written sentence may make sense we have to add the word 'said' (or 'replied' or 'answered' etc.)

Notice also that the speaker's name may be placed before or after the words spoken.

It might help when writing speech if you imagine that the speech marks are the remains of the original ballon:

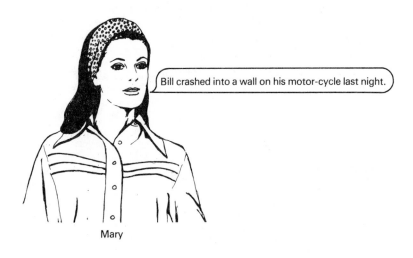

Mary

Mary said, ⌠Bill crashed into a wall on his motor-cycle last night.⌡

Some pupils are often confused about where to place the question-mark in a question sentence occurring in a piece of conversation.

i.e. Should it be:

a John asked, 'What is the time?'

or

b John asked, 'What is the time'?

To find the answer, think back to the balloon. This sentence would appear thus:

John

The question-mark, as you can see, is *inside the balloon*. When written, therefore, it must be placed *inside the speech marks*.

i.e. John asked, 'What is the time?'

Another problem appears when a sentence of speech is broken for some reason – by the speaker's name and the word 'said', for example.

e.g. We'll have to do better said the Captain if we hope to win on Saturday.

How should that sentence be punctuated? If we 'draw' the sentence it should become obvious:

When written this becomes –

'We'll have to do better,' said the Captain, 'if we hope to win on Saturday.'

Should the word 'if' begin with a capital letter or not? This is a question that confuses many pupils. If you look at the balloon you will see which is correct.

Having thought about what you are doing, punctuate the following, putting in capital letters, full-stops, quotation (speech) marks, commas and question marks where necessary.

a at the zoo jack saw elephants lions tigers and bears

b i put the book on the table said ann

c we packed oranges pears apples and plums in the boxes

d barbara who always achieved good marks was absent during the examination

e will you be there tonight asked susan

f if you look now said matthew you will see a kingfisher near the river

g he searched the parks the cinemas the theatres and the amusement arcades but failed to find the boy

h when you arrive said the teacher you must report to the assembly hall

i you will have to pay for four newspapers one magazine three comics and some sweets said the shop-keeper

j mr jones who owned a hardware shop bought a new car

Punctuate this passage:

on friday the circus which came every year arrived at the village green causing great excitement amongst the school population especially interested was tommy smith i go to the circus every year he told his friends so do i said billy tompson but we go in the dear seats his words annoyed tommy i dont care he said he *did* care really of course if only his father who had to work away from the village could earn more money tommy too would be able to sit in the more expensive seats wherever he sat however he intended enjoying the parade of horses elephants dogs the cages of lions and tigers and all the performers before the exciting acts began anyway said tommy im going to go on the trapeze right up there billy looked in the direction indicated by tommy then he lowered his gaze and looked closely at the smaller boy and im going to be a lion-tamer he said

Reports

Reports giving information are written and read daily. . . .

1 REPORT ON NUMBER 5, COVRUM GARDENS

The house is a semi-detached residence, built in 1929. It comprises three bedrooms and a bathroom on the upper floor. There are two large reception rooms and a small kitchen on the ground floor. The front garden is extremely small, but this is compensated for by a very long, though narrow, rear garden.

The property is in need of extensive repairs and complete re-decoration before it will be once again habitable. The floors in both reception rooms are rotted to such an extent that their total replacement is essential. Every window frame will have to be replaced, as will the door leading to the rear garden. Much of the plumbing is ancient, though the bathroom has been modernised to some extent. A low-flush suite would be an improvement, however.

Both gardens, it seems, have been neglected for a number of years.

2 CONFERENCE REPORT

The conference assembled for dinner on Friday evening, 7th March. After the meal the members went to the main hall where the panel of speakers introduced themselves. A short introductory talk followed and the session ended at ten o'clock.

The first session on Saturday morning began at nine o'clock, and the lecture – on general emergencies – lasted until coffee was served at eleven o'clock. This was followed by a film – SEA RESCUE – and an interesting discussion on points raised in the film.

During the afternoon a visit was made to a local RAF station where rescue equipment was on show. The members of the conference were treated to a display by the RAF Rescue Team. . . .

3 MALLEY FEVER

A team of scientists have returned from the mountains of Mid-Wales where they have spent the past two years investigating outbreaks of Malley Fever. The disease, which appears to affect only those living in remote and hilly areas, is never fatal, but it does cause great inconvenience to the sufferer. Legs and arms remain extremely weak for up to ten days – and there is constant headache. The illness leaves the patient as suddenly as it begins, and there seem to be no after-effects.

The scientists are still secretive about their findings, but it is known that they concentrated their attentions on stagnant pools and areas where sheep congregate in large numbers.

(This report is, of course, completely fictitious)

In each of the above extracts from reports information is given. That is the purpose of all reports – to give information accurately, clearly and concisely.

Some of the following reports require considerable research (i.e. reading about the subject and/or paying attention in lessons) before being written. Remember that the reports are not meant to be examples of 'beautiful' English, written to excite, frighten, please etc. They are meant to give information – simply, correctly and in *good* English.

a Describe a house and its grounds for an estate agent who is to sell the property.

b Describe a house that should be condemned because it is in such a poor condition.

c Write a report, describing a park that is soon to be opened to the public.

d Write a report for a magazine, describing a building of particular interest.

e Write a report which Charles Dickens might have composed, describing a work-house of his time.

f Write a report from Florence Nightingale, describing the hospitals of her day.

g Captain Bligh was the master of a famous ship named the 'Bounty'. His crew mutineed and turned him off the vessel. Write a report of conditions aboard as if you were a member of the crew.

h Write a report, describing hospitals in the time of Joseph Lister.

i Write a report, describing an Elizabethan theatre.

j Write a report, describing life in a Saxon village.

Look at the sketch-map of the 'neighbourhood' on p. 60 and then write the following:

a John, a small child, lives in the house marked B. Explain clearly the shortest and safest route he may take in order to attend Manor School. Give reasons for your answer.

b Mr Clark, an old man, lives in the house marked A. He is being forcibly re-housed and must move to a bungalow in New Estate at the top of Church Road.

    (*i*) Imagine that you are Mr Clark and explain why you do not wish to move, pointing out the advantages you presently enjoy, and the disadvantages attaching to your proposed new home.

    (*ii*) Now imagine that you are a housing official who has to persuade Mr Clark that the move is in his own interest. You will have to describe the new advantages he will find.

    (e.g. He will no longer have to cross a busy road in order to collect his pension from the Post Office.)

c Mr Brown lives in the house marked C and he works in the factory marked X. He wishes to buy another house, having the

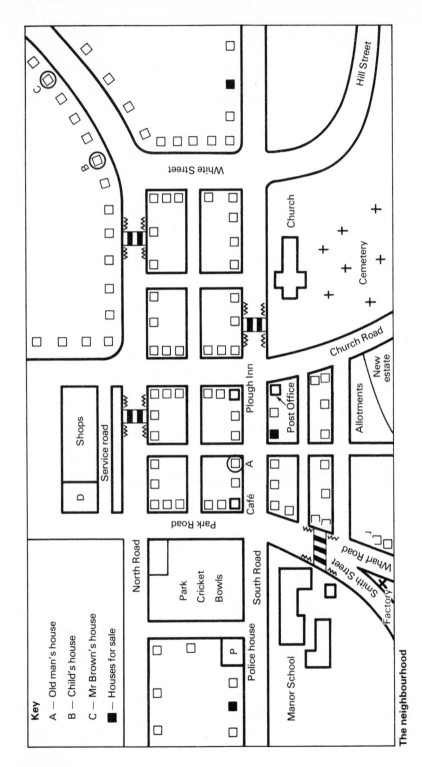

The neighbourhood

Key

A — Old man's house
B — Child's house
C — Mr Brown's house
■ — Houses for sale

60

choice of any of those shaded in. Explain which house you consider to be the most suitable for him, bearing in mind that he is a keen gardener and he plays cricket.

d Imagine that you are P.C. Smith who lives in the police house at the corner of Green Road. Describe the kind of neighbourhood that you patrol, pointing out areas of potential difficulty or trouble.

e Explain clearly how a person might find the Post Office at the corner of Church Road, starting from the shop marked D in North Road. When giving such instructions it is helpful to include obvious 'landmarks' (e.g. the cafe at the corner of Park Road) in order to fix the directions.

f As the lessee (i.e. the holder) of one of the allotments, write a letter to the Headteacher of Manor School, complaining about damage to the gardens, caused by children from the school.

g Write a letter from the Headteacher of Manor School, to the allotment holders, answering the complaints made in 'f' above.

h Write a circular letter from the Vicar of the church in Church Road, explaining that money is required to restore the tower, and asking for volunteers to run sideshows and various stalls at a summer fair.

i As a pupil of Manor School, write a diary for a week, noting people and incidents of interest.

j As an eye-witness, describe the chaos caused by a traffic jam along South Road, explaining the reason for such a hold up.

Dramatic Movement

Mime the following:

a You are waiting on a busy railway station on a windy morning.

b It is a very hot night and you are trying to sleep.

c You are lost in a desert.

d You are a very small child lost in a busy shop.

e You are finding your way through a wood as night falls.

f You are repairing a puncture in your bicycle tyre.

Group work

Improvise these scenes, with or without dialogue:

a Camping with friends.

b A roof-fall while you are in a cave.

c Hay-making.

d A busy outdoor market.

e A scene on a crowded beach.

f A puppet show.

g Decorating a room for an elderly person. Furniture will have to be moved.

h A summer fete.

Look at the sketch-map of a medieval village opposite:

a Imagine that you are a young person living in such a village a thousand years ago and describe the 'three field system'. You will almost certainly have learned about this in your History lessons.

b Describe how you spent a typical day as the daughter or son of a village peasant (serf).

c Imagine that you were the son or daughter of the Lord of the Manor and write an account of what you saw as you rode about the village and its environs.

d Write a diary for a week as it might have been kept by the village priest.

e Imagine that, as a modern person, you fell asleep and woke to find yourself back in time in this village. Write a letter to your parents, explaining how different your life has suddenly become.

f You are producing a television play set in a medieval village. Write a report for the production team, describing the set, mentioning 'modern items' that must not appear. (For instance, characters must not wear wrist-watches as they had not then been invented.)

Dialogues

Remember that when you are writing conversation you should make your speakers say something *interesting* and *worthwhile*.

Write dialogues between:

a Two friends discussing a holiday resort from which they have just returned.

b A visitor and a guide at an exhibition.

c A brother and his sister, comparing the places where they work on Saturdays.

d The leader of a youth club talks to a young person, describing the club and its activities. The teenager is not easily convinced that he/she would like to be a member of the club.

e Two old persons talk about their town as it was when they were

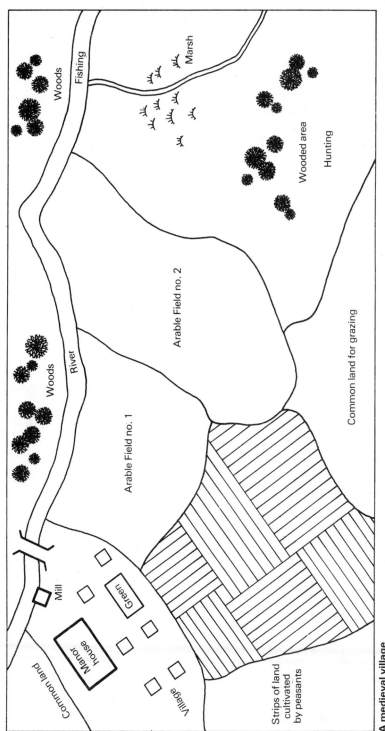

Woods

Fishing

Marsh

Woods

River

Wooded area

Hunting

Arable Field no. 2

Arable Field no. 1

Common land for grazing

Mill

Green

Manor house

Village

Common land

Strips of land cultivated by peasants

A medieval village

63

young. Your imaginations will have to work hard here. Perhaps your grandparents, or some other relatives, will help you.

The following pieces of dialogue are ambitious in that you will need to know a good deal of *correct information* to include in them. Some of the topics you will have heard about in your lessons. If you know little or nothing about other places you should find useful information in the reference books in your school library.

Write dialogues between a newspaper reporter and someone who has just returned from:

a	The Arctic	b	The Sahara Desert
c	Central Australia	d	The Amazon
e	Equatorial Africa	f	Egypt
g	New Guinea	h	Japan
i	New Zealand	j	Alaska

Composition

a Write an account of a visit you have made, either on your own or with a school party: to an agricultural show; to a factory; to a museum etc.

b Write a story in which a place (e.g. a cave, a park, a shed etc.) plays an important part.

c Describe your form-room, as it is now and as you would like it to be.

d Describe your school, as it is now and as you would like it to be.

e You are a member of a committee which proposes to build a holiday camp. Write an account, describing what sort of place you hope it will be.

f Write a story set in a strange land – where even stranger creatures live.

g Write a story in which a world in outer space plays a part.

h Write a story in which the sea-shore is important.

i 'The derelict coal-mine was a frightening place in daylight. At night . . .' Continue this story.

j Write a story set on a village green on a hot afternoon.

k Describe the scene from the window of a country cottage on a cold morning after it has snowed.

l Describe a windy day in the city.

m Write a description of a scene you remember from your holidays.

n Describe the school assembly hall which has been 'dressed up' for a special occasion.

o 'The strange object on the moors.' Write a story suggested by these words.

p Describe either an amusing or an embarrassing incident.

q You act as a guide for a visitor to your school. Describe the visit and the visitor.

Compose any piece of writing suggested by this photograph:

Discussions

When discussing a subject, either orally or in writing, you should try to see that there are usually 'two sides to a question'. Think, for example, of the school rules about which many pupils complain at one time or another. If you write out a list of *all* the rules in your school you might be surprised to discover that there are not so many as you imagined.

Having made your list, see if you can find a good reason for the existence of each.

e.g. *RULE:* Pupils and members of staff must walk along the left-hand sides of corridors.

REASON: Walking always on the left-hand sides of the corridors will reduce the risk of people colliding with each other.

Either *i*) write about the following, or *ii*) discuss as a group:

a Space exploration is a waste of money!

b Keeping animals in zoos! Cruelty or kindness?

c Reading books in this technological age is a waste of time.

d We must stop inventing.

e Pupils should be allowed to leave school at the age of fifteen if they wish.

f Advertising should be banned.

g Holidays have become far too important today.

h Football hooliganism – a cure?

i The motor car does not serve us. *We* serve *it*!

j Our National Health Service.

k Equality between men and women cannot really exist.

l Communities of the future.

m Smoking should be banned by law.

n The modern child is spoilt and his initiative dulled.

o We can no longer afford to be amateur sportsmen.

p We are all responsible for the hungry nations of the world.

q Motor-cycles should be outlawed.

r There is no place for voluntary service in the modern world.

s Every child should be taught to swim.

t Housewives should be paid regular wages.

u A man he was, to all the country dear,
And passing rich with forty pounds a year;
Remote from town he ran his Godly race,
Nor e'er had changed, nor wished to change his place.

Oliver Goldsmith

This man was contented. Are you? Do you ever feel that you would like to 'change your place'? If so – what would you do?

v There's a place and means for every man alive.

William Shakespeare

What do you think this statement means? Do you agree?

w The old order changeth, yielding place to new.

Alfred Lord Tennyson

Is the world about you changing? What do adults feel about this? Do you think older people long for the worlds of their youth? Why? Will you be the same when you grow up?

Projects

a You have been given a large amount of money with which to build a social centre in your neighbourhood. Describe the place you wish to build. Draw some plans, and describe the proposed decorations. Include letters to and from anyone who would be concerned in the administration of it.

b Do the same as for (a) – but for a centre for elderly people.

c Our Town! Each person in the group takes one aspect about

which to write. (e.g. shops; hotels; museums; transport; places of entertainment etc.). Completed efforts might be bound in a folder, entitled 'Guide To . . .'

d A holiday brochure. This might be real or imaginary.

e 'A Guide To Britain's Homes Of Interest' might be compiled. This might be real or imaginary.

f Places that affect you. A varied folder might be produced in which is described places that have some kind of affect upon the writers: e.g. a dentist's waiting-room; a certain church; a social meeting-place; a particular garden; a town centre; a quiet back-water.)

Compose any piece of writing that this photograph suggests:

Compose any pieces of writing that these quotations suggest:

a ... on the French coast the light
  Gleams and is gone.
                    From *Dover Beach* by **Matthew Arnold**

b The man that hath not music in himself
  Nor is not mov'd with concord of sweet sounds,
  Is fit for treasons, stratagems, and spoils.
              From *The Merchant of Venice* by **William Shakespeare**

c All in a hot and copper sky,
  The bloody sun, at noon,
  Right up above the mast did stand,
  No bigger than the moon.
          From *The Rime of the Ancient Mariner* by **S. T. Coleridge**

d A man ... is so in the way in a house.
                                      Elizabeth Gaskell

e I remember, I remember,
  The house where I was born.
                                      Thomas Hood

Sets for Plays

Most modern plays have 'sets' or backgrounds against which the action takes place. The following might be the instructions given to the producer of a play entitled 'Blackbeard The Pirate':

Act 1, Scene 1
To the right of the stage may be seen an entrance to a cave in a pile of rocks. Bushes conceal part of the entrance. Outside the cave, on the ground, are several small barrels, pieces of wood, and boulders of varying sizes. A row of stunted trees form a background, stretching from the rocks in which the cave is situated to the other side of the stage. At the front of the platform and to the left an old rowing-boat is drawn up and two men are busy carrying out repairs on it.

Write descriptions for 'sets' for plays that might have the following titles. Keep your instructions simple and create only one set for each play:

a The Haunted Castle.
b Accident.
c The Old Schoolroom.
d Summer Picnic.
e Challenge of the Rocks.
f Weekend Camp.
g The Forester's Hut.
h Alone On An Island.
i The Highwayman.
j Mystery At The Garage.

4 SEEING

You have now had a good deal of practice in writing – and you have spent time concentrating on the creation of *people*, or *characters*, describing *places* and remembering your *senses*. Now, for a while, you are to concentrate on describing what you *see*.

Many people spend a great deal of time sitting in front of their television sets. Quite possibly you do, but do you simply *look* at what is going on, or do you *see* what is taking place? This is true not only of television, however, but true of so much of our lives. We move about the streets of the city, the lanes of the country, with our eyes open – but how much do we really *see*? Is there any difference between *looking* and *seeing*?

Read this piece of conversation:

'We had a wonderful holiday. We went to Spain and enjoyed two weeks of glorious sunshine.'

'You liked it there?'

'Oh, yes. Never been before, but we intend going again.'

'What did you do with yourselves?'

'Lazed on the beach all day, from early morning till it was dark. We had a swim every day, of course. What do you think of my tan?'

'Very good . . . but do you mean that you stayed in one place for the whole fortnight?'

'Of course!'

'You didn't go and *see* something of the country?'

'What for? We had the sun, the beach, the sea. What else would we want?'

Obviously the holiday-makers saw the sky, the sea, the sand, people, boats and so on, but they appear to have done little else with their eyes. They did not go and really take *notice* of places and things.

Now read this fable:

A crow, being very thirsty, flew over the countryside searching for water. Finally she saw something shining far below. It was water in the bottom of a tall pitcher. At once the crow flew down and stood on the rim of the vessel.

Alas! The neck of the jar was too narrow to allow the bird to thrust - her head down to reach the water. Having failed to reach the liquid, she next tried to push over the pitcher, but in vain, for it was too heavy.

What was she to do?

Lying nearby were pebbles. Seizing one of these, she dropped it into the pitcher. This was followed by another and another until the level of the water rose high enough for the bird to be able to drink.

From *Aesop's Fables*

In that story there is no description of scenery, of the crow, of the pitcher. We are merely told that *there was a crow, there was a pitcher*, and *there was some water*. There is no description of the countryside.

In the following lines, taken from the play *Macbeth* by William Shakespeare, Banquo and his son, Fleance, are talking together:

BANQUO How goes the night, boy?

FLEANCE The moon is down. I have not heard the clock.

BANQUO And she goes down at twelve.

FLEANCE I take it, 'tis later, sir.

BANQUO Hold, take my sword. There's husbandry in heaven.
Their candles are all out.

Shakespeare had little or no scenery and no stage-lighting, the plays being performed in open-air theatres during the hours of daylight. It was sometimes necessary, therefore, for the characters to tell the audience where and when a scene was taking place.

What do we learn from the above passage? It is night and there is no moon. Although Fleance has not heard the midnight clock strike, it is probably later than that, as the moon has gone 'down' and it does so at twelve. Banquo is armed.

Can you explain the lines –

'There's husbandry in heaven. Their candles are all out!'?

Read the following extract:

London. Michaelmas Term lately over, and the Lord Chancellor sitting in Lincoln's Inn Hall. Implacable November weather. As much mud in the streets, as if the waters had but newly retired from the face of the earth, and it would not be wonderful to meet a Megalosaurus, forty feet long or so, waddling like an elephantine lizard up Holborn Hill. Smoke lowering down from the chimney-pots, making a soft black drizzle, with flakes of soot in it as big as full-grown snow-flakes – gone into mourning, one might imagine, for the death of the sun. Dogs undistinguishable in mire. Horses scarcely better; splashed to their very blinkers. Foot passengers jostling one another's umbrellas, in a general infection of ill-temper, and losing their foothold at street-corners, where tens of thousands of foot passengers have been slipping and sliding since the day broke (if the day ever broke), adding new deposits to the crust upon crust of mud, sticking at those points tenaciously to the pavement, and accumulating at compound interest.

Fog everywhere. Fog up the river, where it flows among green aits and meadows; fog down the river, where it rolls defiled among the tiers of shipping, and the waterside pollutions of a great (and dirty) city. Fog on the Essex marshes, fog on the Kentish heights. Fog creeping into the cabooses of collier-brigs; fog lying out on the yards, and hovering in the rigging of great ships; fog drooping on the gunwales of barges and small boats. Fog in the eyes and throats of ancient Greenwich pensioners, wheezing by the firesides of their wards; fog in the stem and bowl of the afternoon pipe of the wrathful skipper, down in his close cabin; fog cruelly pinching the toes and fingers of his shivering little 'prentice boy on deck. Chance people on the bridges peeping over the parapets into a nether sky of fog, with fog all round them, as if they were up in a balloon, and hanging in the misty clouds.

Gas looming through the fog in divers places in the streets, much as the sun may, from the spongy fields, be seen to loom by husbandmen and ploughboy. Most of the shops lighted two hours before their time – as the gas seems to know, for it has a haggard and unwilling look.

The raw afternoon is rawest, and the dense fog is densest, and the muddy streets are muddiest, near that leaden-headed old obstruction, appropriate ornament for the threshold of a leaden-headed old corporation: Temple Bar. And hard by Temple Bar, in Lincoln's Inn Hall, at the very heart of the fog, sits the Lord High Chancellor in his High Court of Chancery.

From *Bleak House* by **Charles Dickens**

a What effect has the repetition of the word 'fog'?

b Do you find that passage effective as the opening of a novel? Give reasons for your answer.

c See if you can write a similar description – but make it of a bright, sunny day.

RAIN IN SUMMER

How beautiful is the rain!
After the dust and heat,
In the broad and fiery street,
In the narrow lane,
How beautiful is the rain!
How it clatters along the roofs,
Like the tramp of hoofs!

How it gushes and struggles out
From the throat of the overflowing spout!
Across the windy pane
It pours and pours;
And swift and wide,
With a muddy tide,
Like a river down the gutter roars
The Rain, the welcome rain!

H. W. Longfellow

a What are your feelings about rain? Does rain affect you in a particular way?

b Write a 'dismal' picture of a rainy day.

c Now see if you can describe a 'bright' rainy day.

Describing Words

Look at this sentence:

The boy entered the house.

It is a sentence, being a group of words that makes complete sense.

We can make it a little more interesting by adding words that tell us more, or *describe*, the nouns 'boy' and 'house'.

e.g. The *untidy* boy entered the *derelict* house.

Or we can write:

The boy, *who was untidy*, entered the derelict house.

Or:

The untidy boy entered the house *which was derelict*.

Or:

The boy, *who was untidy*, entered the house *which was derelict*.

Make the following sentences more interesting by placing describing words before the nouns which are underlined:

a The man ran away.

b We climbed the mountain.

c Ahead of us was the castle.

d Philip bought the house.

e They entered the forest.

f The man sold a car.

g Two women went to see the school.

h The dog took the bone.

i The woman knitted a garment.

j The girl opened the gate.

When employing describing words (i.e. adjectives) use them *sparingly*, and choose those that are most apt for the particular occasion. Remember to make use of your thesaurus.

Adjectives are not the only describing words that may be used to make your writing more vivid.

You will remember, of course, that a sentence contains a *noun* (or a pronoun) and a *verb*, a word which tells us what is *done* in the sentence.

e.g. The man *walked*.

The verb in that sentence is the word 'walked', telling us what the man *did*.

That sentence may be made a little more interesting by adding a word which tells us more about the word 'walked'.

e.g. The man walked *slowly*.

The man walked *quickly*.

These describing words are known as *adverbs* (they *add* something to the verb) and they usually tell us *how, when* or *where* something is done.

Underline the *adverbs* in these sentences:

a The UFO appeared suddenly.

b The baby cried bitterly.

c The dogs ate ravenously.

d Savagely he blew the horn.

e Mrs Jones sewed neatly.

f The thunder rolled furiously.

Sometimes a group of words may be used to do the work of an adverb.

e.g. The dog ran *quickly*.

This may also be expressed:

The dog ran *at a quick pace*.

e.g. The wind blew *fiercely*.

This may also be expressed:

The wind blew *with great ferocity*.

Make the following sentences more interesting by

(*i*) including an adverb

(*ii*) including groups of words that do the work of adverbs:

a Mary waited . . .

b The rain fell . . .

c The lion attacked . . .

d Dawn broke . . .

e All the women arrived . . .

f Margaret sighed . . .

g Billy and Tommy played . . .

h The bell sounded . . .

i The man drove the car . . .

j The siren wailed . . .

Now look at this sentence:

The boy rode his motor-cycle.

We can make that sentence more interesting by adding –

(*i*) An adjective, or a group of words that do the work of an adjective, to the noun 'boy'; and *(ii)* An adverb, or a group of words that do the work of an adverb, to the verb 'rode'.

e.g. The *foolish* boy rode his motor-cycle *carelessly*.
The boy, *who was foolish*, rode his motor-cycle *in a careless manner*.

e.g. Jack rowed the boat . . .
may be written –
Jack rowed the *new* boat *skilfully*.
Or   Jack rowed the boat, *which was new, in a skilful manner*.

Make the following sentences more interesting by adding single describing words, or groups of describing words, either to the underlined nouns, or the verbs, or to both:

a The girl cried.
b The wind moaned in the trees.
c The boys shouted.
d Jack carried a parcel.
e The bear growled.

Read the following extract, noticing the use of describing words:

The jungle was wide and full of twittering, rustlings, murmurs, and sighs.

Suddenly it all ceased, as if someone had shut a door.

Silence.

A sound of thunder.

Out of the mist, one hundred yards away, came Tyrannosaurus Rex.

'No!' whispered Eckels. 'No. No!'

It came on great oiled, resilient, striding legs. It towered thirty feet above half of the trees, a great evil god, folding its delicate watchmaker's claws, close to its oily reptilian chest. Each lower leg was a piston, a thousand pounds of white bone, sunk in thick ropes of muscle, sheathed over in a gleam of pebbled skin like the mail of a terrible warrior. Each thigh was a ton of meat, ivory, and steel mesh. And from the great breathing cage of the upper body those two delicate arms dangled out front, arms with hands which might pick up and examine men like toys, while the snake neck coiled. And the head itself, a ton of sculptured stone, lifted easily upon the sky. Its mouth gaped, exposing a fence of teeth like daggers. Its eyes rolled, ostrich eggs, empty of all expression save hunger. It closed its mouth in a deathly grin. It ran, its pelvic bones crushing aside trees and bushes, its taloned feet clawing damp earth, leaving prints six inches deep wherever it settled its weight. It ran with a gliding ballet step, far too poised and balanced for its ten tons. It moved into a sunlit arena warily, its beautifully reptile hands feeling the air.

'My God!' Eckels twitched his mouth. 'It could reach up and grab the moon.'

From *A Sound of Thunder* by **Ray Bradbury**

Oral work

INDIVIDUAL WORK:

Describe the following, trying to make your listeners 'see' the picture you are painting:

a My bedroom.

b Our garden.

c My favourite outfit.

d A building I like.

e A building I dislike.

f A visit to . . .

g A dream.

h Our old car.

i My village (city).

j My hobby.

WORK IN PAIRS:

Invent conversations between a newspaper reporter and a traveller who has:

a Returned from a Red Indian camp of the past.

b Explored the Congo.

c Found a hitherto unknown Pacific Island.

d Been to the Moon.

WORK IN GROUPS:

a A travel agent tries to encourage customers to visit various places by 'painting' word pictures for them. The customers, in turn, dwell on memories of last year's holiday.

b People from different places are travelling on a coach. Each sings the praises of his/her own neighbourhood.

c A public meeting has been called to protest against a proposed new road which is to cut across rich farmland and some areas of outstanding beauty.

d Several people have seen a strange animal, or an 'unearthly being' on the moors. Each tries to describe it to the police.

Written work

Write the following descriptive passages, making them as vivid as possible:

a A street scene very early in the morning.

b A thunder-storm in the mountains.

c A hot afternoon by the lake.

d Sunset in the city.

e Early morning at the site of a circus.

The suggestions above mention no people. Re-write the passages, but including people who must also be described, e.g.:

    (*i*) a might include a milkman.

    (*ii*) b might include a mountain guide.

    (*iii*) c might include a fisherman.

    (*iv*) d might include an old person.

    (*v*) e might include a circus performer.

Compose any piece of writing that is suggested to you by this photograph.

Read this piece of dialogue. Notice that the action is mixed with the conversation.

The two men entered the cafe and sat down. Sam, the heavy-looking character, rubbed his stubbly chin between a thick thumb and forefinger as he looked thoughtfully at the menu.

'What you fancy to eat, Ted?' he asked. 'Not much choice.'

The other looked up from the newspaper he was reading, that he seemed always to be reading. 'Wouldn't mind a sandwich, but I don't reckon I'll bother. I could do with a drink, though.'

'Coffee?'

'Tea. With plenty of sugar.'

Sam sniffed miserably, closed the menu card and nodded to the waitress who had been hovering hopefully since they had entered.

'Two teas, please, Miss,' he said. 'And a cheese sandwich.' He glanced across at his companion. 'Sure you won't have a sandwich, Ted? I'm paying.'

Ted grinned. 'In that case – I will,' he said.

The next piece of dialogue is different. You will notice that words like 'he said' and 'she said' are not used, yet it is easy to know who is speaking.

A woman, Mrs Carter, is giving evidence in a court of law. Here she is being questioned by a barrister:

'You actually saw the crime being committed, Mrs Carter?'

'Yes.'

'When?'

'It was ten minutes past seven o'clock on the morning of 17th June.'

'You seem to be very sure of the time and the date!'

'I should be. I was on my way to catch the 7.15 train to Brighton, and I checked the time as the station came into sight.'

'And you're certain of the date?'

'Positive. It was the first day of my holidays.'

'Will you, please, tell us exactly what you saw at ten minutes past seven on that Monday morning?'

'As I turned into Station Road, which was quite deserted at the time, a green car passed me. The driver seemed to be in a hurry. The car stopped outside a shop.'

'A jeweller's shop?'

'Yes.'

'And?'

'And a man, wearing a stocking over his face, got out and threw something through the window. Then he grabbed something from inside the window, got back into the car and drove off.'

'Did you notice if there was anyone else in the car?'

'I'm sorry, I didn't.'

Write the following interviews, introducing into them information that is relevant to the place mentioned. For example, if you choose 'The Canals' you should mention locks, lock-keepers, tunnels, long-boats and so on. Should you decide to write about Switzerland you would probably mention mountains, watches, cable-cars and skiing.

The conversations should be between you and a friend who has just returned from a holiday in:

a North Wales.

b The Lake District.

c The Highlands of Scotland.

d Cornwall.

e Switzerland.

f On the Canals.

g Any seaside resort.

h A Mediterranean cruise.

Punctuation

Generally speaking school pupils are parsimonious (sparing) in their use of the apostrophe.

As with other punctuation marks, we do not use them when we are speaking:

e.g. Jack's coat lay on the floor.

If you speak that sentence everyone who hears you knows that the coat *belongs to* Jack. It is his *possession*. When the sentence is written we show that the coat *belongs to* Jack (i.e. is one of his *possessions*) by using an apostrophe, as shown in the example above.

Examiners, and teachers of English, constantly complain that too many candidates and pupils rarely use the apostrophe – and when they *do* include it they frequently mis-use it.

The rules for using the apostrophe are really quite simple.

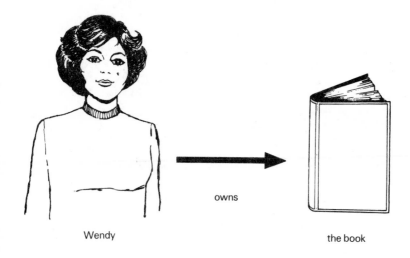

Wendy   owns   the book

The book *belongs to* Wendy.
It is her *possession*.
It is *her* book.
It is *Wendy's* book.

How do we arrive at the final version (i.e. 'It is Wendy's book') when we use the apostrophe?

1 Name the person (or thing) to whom the object belongs:
   Wendy

2 Where the gap was in the sketch –

78

Wendy

book

we place the apostrophe –
Wendy'
and add an 's' –
Wendy's
The apostrophe shows that the book *belongs to* Wendy.
It is her *possession*.

Rewrite the following by filling in the gaps and adding an apostrophe in each case:

a The tail *belonging to* the dog.   The . . . tail.
b The tent *belonging to* the boy.   The . . . tent.
c The crown *belonging to* the king.   The . . . crown.
d The doll *belonging to* the girl.   The . . . doll.
e The car *belonging to* Jim.   . . . car.
f The keys *belonging to* the teacher.   The . . . keys.
g The hangbag *belonging to* Jane.   . . . handbag.
h The daughter *belonging to* the master.   The . . . daughter.
i The newspaper *belonging to* the old man. The . . . newspaper.
j The knitting-needles *belonging to* the mother.
                                    The . . . knitting needles.

Now write the following, each to include an apostrophe showing possession.

A sentence which mentions:

a a model belonging to Billy.
b the paw of a dog.

c a scarf belonging to an old lady.
d the foot of an elephant.
e a drill belonging to a dentist.
f the red nose of a clown.
g the answer-paper belonging to a candidate.
h a cap belonging to Mark.
i the anchor belonging to a ship.
j the club belonging to a golfer.

Check that:
(*i*) you have used the apostrophe correctly, and
(*ii*) your sentence is, in fact, a sentence.

If we wish to show that something belongs to someone whose name already ends in an 's' (e.g. Mrs Jones) we simply add another 's' after the apostrophe.

> e.g. The book belonging to Mrs Jones may be written as
> *Mrs Jones's book.*

When we wish to show that something belongs to more than one person:

> e.g. the school belonging to the girls

we write the plural form of the possessor (i.e. in this case 'girls') and add the apostrophe *after* the 's'.

> i.e. *the girls' school.*

Rewrite the following by filling in the gaps and adding apostrophes:

a The dresses *belonging to* the babies.   The . . . dresses.
b The shop *belonging to* Mrs Williams.   Mrs . . . shop.
c The cars *belonging to* the doctors.   The . . . cars.
d The Church of Saint Peter.   Saint . . . Church.
e The den of the lions.   The . . . den.

Note that the word 'of' in the last two examples means *belonging to.*

Punctuate the following passage, putting in the capital letters, full-stops, question-marks, commas, quotation-marks and apostrophes:

the two boys who were the best of friends set off for the lake early alan carried both the fishing-rods his own and billys think well catch that old pike asked billy as they stopped at the waters edge alan grinned i dont see why not he said if old mr wilkins can land a pike so can we suddenly he stopped talking he pointed towards the middle of the lake what is it asked alan it looks like a boat billy nodded it is a boat he said but theres nobody on it is there the small craft was indeed deserted but the lake itself had an occupant floating several yards from the shore was a dark bulky object

Once again – check that your sentences are sentences, that you have used quotation-marks to enclose speech, that you have started a new line for each speaker and that all the other rules of punctuation have been observed.

To show possession is not the only function of the apostrophe. It is also used to show that a letter (or letters) has been omitted.

We write conversation in Direct Speech and, in order to make it sound convincing, we use contractions – i.e. shortened forms of certain words.

e.g. *I'll* go this afternoon.
instead of –
    I shall go this afternoon.
    e.g. "I *do not* like the soup,' said Ted –
may become
    'I don't like the soup,' said Ted.

Rewrite the following, making contractions where possible:

a 'I did not put the cake there,' protested Gail.

b The boys said, 'We cannot finish this work in time.'

c 'I am sure that the last 'bus has gone,' said Mr Roberts.

d 'She will be late again today,' said June's mother.

e 'Did not you say that we should meet outside the cinema?' asked Jennifer.

Punctuate this passage, putting all marks of punctuation in the correct places:

well said june weve arrived but where is everybody else she looked about her and noticed that the platform was deserted except for one porter two sleepy dogs penny and herself maybe were early suggested penny though not with confidence she glanced at the delicate watch on her wrist ten o'clock we cant be early can we june always a restless girl pushed her case against a trolley and strolled along the platform it was the tone of her friends voice that caused her to halt abruptly and turn back penny – you know what weve done the expression on junes face was evidence enough of her inner feelings weve got the right time she said but the wrong day its next tuesday we are going not today.

Definitions

Considerable skill in the use of words is necessary in order to write a definition; that is, to explain in a few words only what is meant by a particular item, for example, or an occupation:

e.g. *Define a veterinary surgeon.*

A veterinary surgeon is a medical person who deals with ailments and injuries in all creatures other than human beings.

In order to write a definition:

a State the 'family' to which the thing to be defined belongs.

    i.e. veterinary surgeon – a medical person.

b Explain how the object is different from other objects in the same family. In this case show how a veterinary surgeon differs from other 'medical persons'.

    i.e. – deals with creatures other than humans.

Write brief definitions of the following:

a a pharmacist.	b a ruler.
c a cricket ball.	d a dog kennel.
e a sock.	f a saucer.
g a camera.	h a violin.
i a park.	j a flag.
k a poacher.	l a bread knife.
m a nail.	n a holiday chalet.
o a hammer.	p a rug.
q a text book.	r an optician.
s a botanist.	t a lollipop.

Paragraphs

Long written passages should be broken up into paragraphs. Doing so gives the piece 'eye appeal', making it easier for the reader to assimilate what is being presented, because each paragraph should contain *only one main idea*.

Look at this example:

We first saw the lake at dawn on the Sunday morning. It was the enormous size of it that impressed us at once. The mighty stretch of water, grey and dull under a leaden sky, ran away from us until it united with the purple hills more than three miles distant. Nothing, not bird, not craft, nor man moved on the surface that was slightly ruffled by a breeze which seemed to be rising far behind us in the valley from which we had just emerged.

The main idea in that passage was stated in the first sentence.

Using one main idea for each, write descriptive paragraphs suggested by:

a fog b clouds c moonlight d wind e fire
f smoke g shadows h sunlight i the sea j frost in moonlight

Once again, read several newspapers, noting the various styles used. Then write the following reports, remembering: *one main idea – one paragraph.*

a A storm has ravaged the countryside, uprooting trees and destroying barns.

b A hurricane strikes a small town one night.

c Dense fog causes chaos in a large industrial town.

d A rescue-team reaches a wrecked aeroplane in the mountains.

Look at the sketch-map on p. 84 showing a rail journey:

a Describe what you see on your left-hand side as you travel from village A to village B.

b Describe what you see on your left-hand side on the return trip.

c Write a diary for a week as it might have been kept by the train driver on this route.

d Write about your daily life – your work and your leisure time – as if you were living at the farm.

e You have been sent to examine the neighbourhood in which the boating lake is situated to see whether or not it might be suitable to develop as a leisure area. Having considered all the factors, write your report.

f Write a story in which the railway tunnel plays an important part.

g Write a diary for a week as it might be kept by the lock-keeper on the canal-side.

h Write an account, for a local magazine, of the cricket match as witnessed by a spectator.

Planning

Read this passage:

Jack spoke.

'We've got to decide about being rescued.'

There was a buzz. One of the small boys, Henry, said that he wanted to go home.

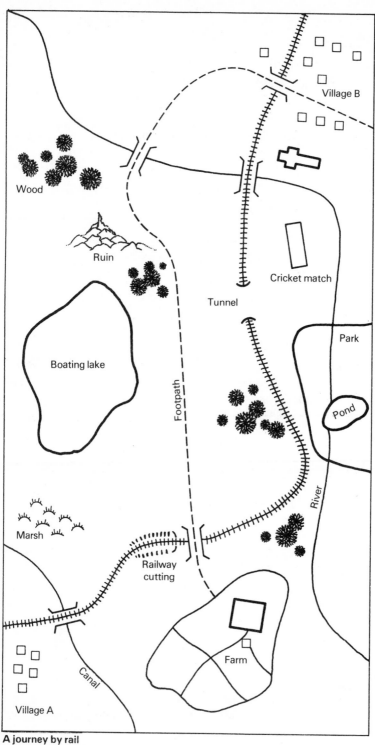

A journey by rail

'Shut up,' said Jack absently. He lifted the conch. 'Seems to me we ought to have a chief to decide things.'

'A chief! A chief!'

'I ought to be chief,' said Jack with simple arrogance, 'because I'm chapter chorister and head boy. I can sing C sharp.'

Another buzz.

'Well then,' said Jack. 'I –'

He hesitated. The dark boy, Roger, stirred at last and spoke up.

'Let's have a vote.'

'Yes.'

'Vote for a chief!'

'Let's vote –'

This toy of voting was almost as pleasing as the conch. Jack started to protest but the clamour changed from the general wish for a chief to an election by acclaim of Ralph himself. None of the boys could have found good reason for this; what intelligence had been shown was traceable to Piggy while the most obvious leader was Jack. But there was a stillness about Ralph as he sat that marked him out: there was his size, and attractive appearance; and most obsurely, yet most powerfully, there was the conch. The being that had blown that, had sat waiting for them on the platform with the delicate thing balanced on his knees, was set apart.

'Him with the shell.'

'Ralph! Ralph!'

'Let him be chief with the trumpet-thing.'

Ralph raised a hand for silence.

'All right. Who wants Jack for chief?'

With dreary obedience the choir raised their hands.

'Who wants me?'

Every hand outside the choir except Piggy's was raised immediately. Then Piggy, too, raised his hand grudgingly into the air.

Ralph counted.

'I'm chief then.'

From *Lord of the Flies* by **William Golding**

The book – *Lord of the Flies* – is about a group of boys who find themselves on an island with no adults. For a few days they do as they please, but soon the need for organisation becomes apparent. In the passage quoted they realise that they need some kind of leader. They have to *plan* for the future.

Look at the illustration on page 86:

The top diagram shows an empty room, and below it various pieces of furniture. Before the householder placed the furniture in position he *planned* where each piece would go. Even if he did not sketch a plan – as that shown in the lower diagram – he probably made a mental plan.

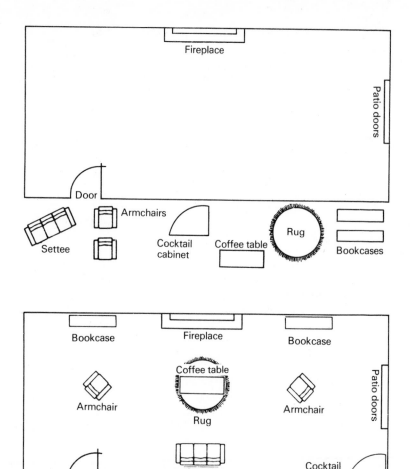

Think of a man who is about to go on holiday. Having decided on his destination, he will *plan* how he will travel, what route he will take, and whether he will break his journey or not. Once he has arrived at the resort he will *plan* how he will spend his time.

Now look at the everyday objects in your room – the television set, an electric fire, a transistor radio, a carpet – everything, in fact. You can be sure that before each was manufactured there was a great deal of *planning*. The book you are now reading was planned. What should it contain? How should it be set out? Every day in every town and city and village people are planning.

The same should be true of you when you start to write. It is not often that someone can produce a *good* piece of creative writing without some kind of planning beforehand, even if it is only jotting down some notes for the order in which it is to be written.

Look at the first suggestion under the heading 'Stories' below – 'You and your friend visit a deserted house'. First you must begin the story by *plunging straight into it*.

e.g. 'As we crept up the drive towards the old house we both thought that we saw movement in an upstairs window. 'It's supposed to be deserted,' whispered Jack. 'Did you see something?'

I told him that I did, but before I could say another word we both had reason to freeze in our tracks. . . .

We must now consider the rest of the tale. That is, we must *plan*. It might go something like this:

b Having seen the tiny movement, the boys hide. Nothing further happens and they find courage. . . .

c to enter the house, which *seems* to be deserted.

d Inside, the house is musty and empty, but on the dusty stairs they see small foot-prints leading upwards.

e They think back to the morning. Near the woods, on the way to the house, they had passed a tramp. Was he now in the house? Would he attack them if he was?

f Finally, after some debate, they go upstairs – which is also deserted. While they are investigating one of the rooms the door slams and they are locked inside. A laugh is heard from outside the door.

g They panic, shout and bang on the door.

h The end of the story.

Preparing a plan allows you to concentrate on the actual task of writing. Without it you could well spend time wondering what to write about next.

Maybe you would like to invent an ending for that story. Or you might prefer to write your own from the beginning.

Before you set out to write anything – be sure to *plan*. You might find the making of such outlines tedious, but you will soon discover that they are more than useful. They are *essential* for good creative writing.

Stories

Write stories suggested by the following, remembering your *senses*:

a You and your friend visit a deserted house.

b You prepare for a visit from a relation you have never seen.

c One evening at dusk you see a strange object in the river.

d An exciting cruise . . .

e 'I never thought it could happen to me . . .

f The night we went to the theatre.

g The new school.

h 'It was a terrifying dream . . . that seemed to be coming true . . .

Look at the sketch-map of the accident opposite.

Facts: As the 'bus B moved away from the 'bus-stop, car A turned off Main Road into Oak Lane and they collided. No one was hurt.

a Describe what happened, as told by:
   (*i*) The 'bus driver.
   (*ii*) The driver of car A.

b Describe what appeared to have happened, as seen by:
   (*i*)   Witness C.
   (*ii*) Witness D.
   (*iii*) Witness E.

c Have you any comment to make on the siting of the 'bus-stop and the pedestrian crossing?

d Write a diary for a week as it might be kept by the 'bus driver.

e Write an account to explain why Witness D was in a hurry to catch the 'bus on that particular morning.

f Write an account of a day in your life as if you were a School Crossing Warden at the pedestrian crossing shown.

Description

When you are asked to write a description of an object you begin as if you were writing a definition. That is, you name the general group to which the object belongs.

e.g. A fountain-pen is an implement with which we write.

Now you describe the appearance and the construction of the object. Make brief notes, putting the details in logical order; that is, make a *plan*.

e.g. An outer, cylindrical barrel, made of plastic of various colours.

Open end closed by nib.

Blunt, open end of nib screwed into open end of rubber sac, other end of which is closed.

Rubber sac enclosed within outer barrel.

Lever in side of barrel presses on rubber sac to expel air.

Nib placed in ink and lever released.

Ink sucked into sac.

Ink flows from inner container through the nib, and on to the page.

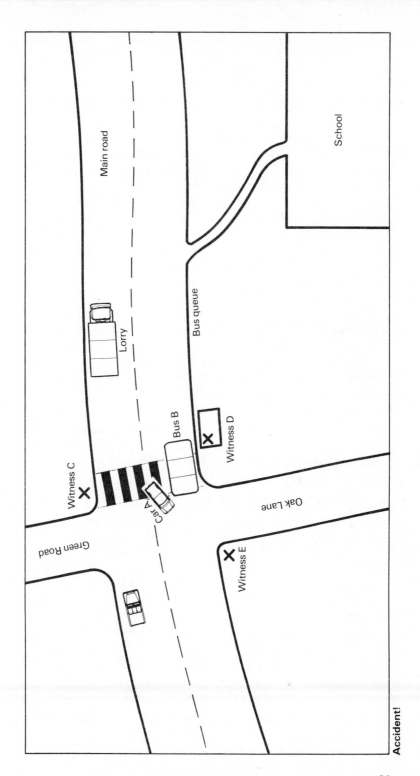

Accident!

When not in use nib is protected by a removable cap of same material as that of barrel.

Cap has clip attached to hold pen securely in pocket.

Now, using the plan, write a concise description of the fountain-pen:

A fountain-pen is an implement with which we write.

It consists of an outer case, closed at one end and made of plastic, which may be of almost any colour. The open end of the case, or barrel as it is known, is closed by a nib. The blunt end of the nib is screwed into the open end of a cylindrical rubber sac, the other end of which is closed. This sac is enclosed within the outer barrel.

Lifting a small lever, which is inserted in the rigid outer barrel, causes the air to be expelled from the inner rubber sac. The nib is immersed in ink, the lever returned to its original position and the ink is sucked in, filling the sac.

In order to write, the operator places the nib on paper and forms words. While this is happening the ink flows very slowly out of the inner container, down the nib and on to the paper.

When not in use the nib is protected by a removable cap which is made of the same material as that used in the outer barrel. This cap usually has a clip attached to it so that the pen may be carried securely in the pocket.

Note that in any piece of factual writing such as that description there is no place for figurative language, no striving to find the most apt imaginative words and phrases. The object is to describe the article clearly and concisely.

Write detailed descriptions of the following:

a a spanner	b a ball-point pen
c a sweeping brush	d a brief-case
e a skate-board	f a thermos-flask
g a test-tube	h a kettle
i a frying-pan	j a protractor
k a wellington boot	l a coffee table
m a crash helmet	n a thermometer
o a pair of sun-glasses	p a calculator

Frequently you are asked how to do something. You have to describe an operation of some kind. As before, the first thing to do is to make a *plan*:

> e.g. *To paint a door*
>
> Gather together the equipment needed – a brush, paint, sandpaper.
>
> Smooth the door and clean it thoroughly.

Apply the paint, using brush.

After applying several brushloads of paint use long upwards strokes, running brush lightly into paint already on door. This will avoid leaving brush marks.

Description:

The equipment required to paint a door consists of a pot of paint, a brush and a piece of sandpaper.

Firstly, the door must be cleaned of all flakes of old paint and then rubbed down with the sandpaper until the surface is smooth. Small holes should be filled in with an appropriate compound, many of which are sold at D.I.Y. shops.

Using a good quality brush, apply paint to the prepared woodwork, taking care not to be too liberal with the application so that 'runs' may be avoided. After each brushful has been rubbed out use long upward strokes, running the brush lightly into the paint you have already put on the door. This operation will help to avoid leaving brush marks in the finished work.

Again, notice that the description is written in plain, matter-of-fact English.

Explain, clearly and concisely, how to perform the following operations:

How:

a to clean your teeth.

b to cash a postal-order.

c to make a telephone call – (i) from your home, (ii) from a public kiosk.

d to sharpen a pencil.

e to mend a puncture in a bicycle tyre.

f to re-pot a plant.

g to press a pair of trousers.

h to clean a window.

i to polish a pair of very dirty shoes.

j to fill a fountain-pen.

k to play a record.

l to work a tape-recorder.

m to replace a broken window.

n to repair a tear in a skirt.

o to use a pedestrian crossing that is controlled by lights.

p to boil an egg.

q to wash and polish a car.

r to wash a blouse by hand.

s to insert a refill in a ball-point pen.

t to make a cup of instant coffee.

Another type of description is involved in the giving of instructions that will enable someone to reach a particular place. We have all been asked at some time how someone can 'get to such and such a place'. Usually our instructions go something like this: 'Take the first left and go along there for half a mile. Then take the third road on your right. Turn sharp left and right again at the cross-roads. Cross over the traffic-lights and then take the first left hand turn. . . .'

At this point we are usually becoming as confused as the person we are trying to help. There *is* a correct way to give instructions:

e.g. Look at the sketch-map and explain how Driver A might get to house B, using the shortest route.

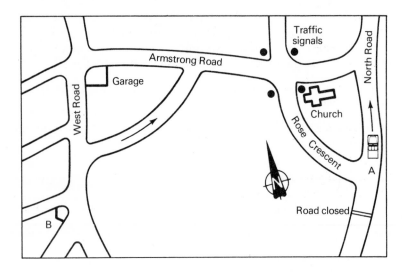

Go along North Road and take the first left turn into Armstrong Road. Continue along Armstrong Road, passing a Church on your left. Go through one set of traffic-lights and drive on until you come to a large garage on a corner. Turn left there, into West Road and stay on that road for about half a mile. Take the third road on your right and you will find House B on the first corner.

Notice that obvious 'landmarks' (i.e. the Church, the traffic-lights and the garage) are mentioned. This helps the driver to fix the directions in his mind.

Written Work

a Perhaps a relation of yours has an unusual occupation. Talk to him/her about it and then write an account of it, making it sound authentic and using correct technical terms, if there are any.

b You have lost a particular object. Write a description of it for the police, giving sufficient detail to prove that it belongs to you.

c Write a description of your pet, explaining how you feed it, keep it clean, house it and what you do with it when you go away on holiday.

d The people in your street are preparing to celebrate some event by having sports, games, a fancy-dress competition and a street-party.

Write (i)   the diary of a child who is eagerly looking forward to the events,

(ii) the diary of the chief organiser,

(iii) a description of the final event – the street-party.

e Look at the sketch-map and explain how the lorry-driver A may reach the Factory B in North Road.

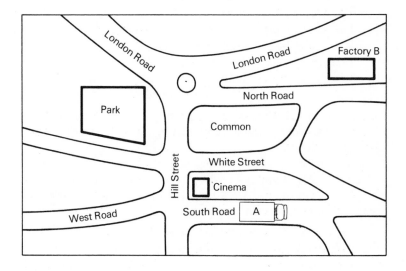

Poetry

A poet is a master craftsman with words. He is economical in his use of them. That is to say, he paints his picture, or makes his point, or re-lives a memory in as few words as possible. While doing so he strives to find the most *apt* and the most *vivid* words.

Read these two poems, preferably aloud:

SLOWLY

Slowly the tide creeps up the sand,
Slowly the shadows cross the land.
Slowly the cart-horse pulls his mile,
   Slowly the old man mounts the stile.
Slowly the hands move round the clock,
Slowly the dew dries on the dock.
Slow is the snail – but slowest of all
   The green moss spreads on the old brick wall.

James Reeves

GALE WARNING

The wind breaks bound, tossing the oak and chestnut,
Whirling the papers at street corners,
The city clerks are harrassed, wrestling head-down:
The gulls are blown inland.

Three slates fall from a roof,
The promenade is in danger:
Inland, the summer fete is postponed,
The British glider record broken.

The wind blows through the City, cleansing,
Whipping the posters from the hoardings,
Tearing the bunting and the banners,
The wind blows steadily, and as it will.

Michael Roberts

Despite the fact that many young people *say* they do not care for poetry, very many of them enjoy reading poems – and even more like *writing* poetry.

Composing poetry is a very personal exercise. If you choose to write lines that rhyme you will possibly find that you have to struggle occasionally to find suitable words, giving the composition an unnatural feel to it.

A Write poems suggested by the following titles:

a Old Man/Woman.	k Sports Day.
b Winter Morning.	l The Man in the Railway Carriage.
c Supermarket.	m Snow in the City.
d The 'Bus Station.	n The Match.
e Goodbye	o Sailing.
f Rain.	p Car-Park.
g Harvest Home.	q Flowers.
h Mountain Stream.	r The Roundabout.
i Coal.	s By the Lake.
j Lonely.	t Postmen.

B Write poems suggested by the following:

a A country scene in moonlight.

b A rowing trip on a lake.

c A sudden storm while you are hill-walking.

d Your thoughts as you look at a rubbish-tip.

e A walk through woods on a warm Autumn day.

f Your feelings as you recall your childhood days.

g The view from the lawn of a house which is close to a beach.

h A thunder-storm while you are alone in the house.

i A school journey.

j A visit to a place of great historical interest.

k Your thoughts when you first see your new pet.

l The sight of a derelict house.

m The city centre on a very hot afternoon.

n A walk through the grounds of a hospital.

o Your thoughts and feelings as you leave school for the last time.

p The scene outside a theatre where a famous 'star' is about to arrive.

q A serious fire in an old building.

r A summer air-display.

s The scene in a busy store.

t The scene in a large junk-yard.

Letters

Write the following letters, making them as interesting as possible:

a To a friend, describing the hospital ward in which you are spending Christmas as a patient.

b You are a member of a group on a field-course in the mountains. Write home, telling your parents about the area and your camp.

c You have been on a school flying trip. In a letter to your parents describe what you saw and how you felt.

d Write a letter home – from a ship which is taking you on an educational cruise.

Diaries

Write entries for a week or two for each of the following:

a The leader of a Polar expedition. Before you begin you should read about such adventures. In your diary you should include notes about the weather, the conditions of various members of your team, food and the lack of it.

b The Captain of a ship. Again, you will need to know something about the life and duty of a ship's Captain. Remember that there are many kinds of ships and that the duties of their Captains will vary.

c The leader of a mountain-rescue team. It is possible that one of your teachers is, or has been, a member of such a team. Some rescues take several days to complete, and a leader might well keep a detailed diary of what the team is doing – step by step. Times are also important in such a record.

d The school log-book . . . by the Headteacher. The log-book is a type of diary in which the Headteacher has to record items that are important to the school. For example, visits by important people; visits by Her Majesty's Inspectors of Schools; appointments of new members of staff; the sending of a pupil to hospital and so on.

e The Mayor of Hamelin. Before attempting this you should read again the poem *The Pied Piper of Hamelin* by Robert Browning.

Compose any piece of writing suggested to you by this photograph:

Compose any pieces of writing that these quotations suggest to you:

> (*i*) The wrinkled sea beneath him crawls:
>   He watches from his mountain walls.
>   **Lord Tennyson**

(*ii*) Day after day, day after day,
We stuck, nor breath nor motion;
As idle as a painted ship
Upon a painted ocean.

S. T. Coleridge

(*iii*) Night coming upon me, I began, with a heavy heart, to consider what would be my lot if there were any ravenous beasts in that country, seeing that at night they always come abroad for their prey.

Daniel Defoe

(*iv*) Now upon the further shore
Lands the voyager at last.

John Ellerton

(*v*) Once a word has been allowed to escape, it cannot be recalled.

Horace

5 CLIMAX

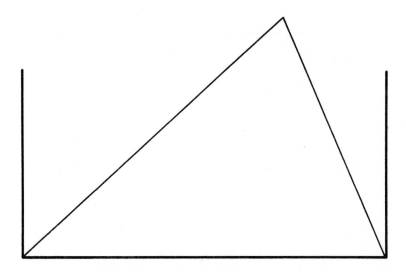

What is the diagram above? A temperature chart? A rainfall gauge?

No!

It is a story. At least – it is the plan of a story – any good story.

Look again:

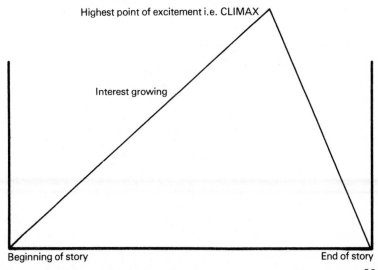

Every good story has a *climax*. That is, it rises in excitement to its highest point. Then the level of excitement drops *suddenly* and the story ends.

Look at this example:

A man has run away from a hospital where he has been under observation. After his escape the doctors discover that he has a very contagious disease – say – plague, which can kill many thousands of people. The man does not know all this. So – the great hunt for him is on. He *must* be found, firstly because he himself will die and, secondly, because he can spread the disease quickly.

The search for him grows more and more exciting and several times he is almost caught, but each time he manages to slip away. This causes the tension to grow until he is finally found. His capture is the *climax*. Following this climax the story ends very quickly.

Read these extracts:

The scene: *A cavern. In the middle – a boiling cauldron. Thunder and lightning. Enter Three Witches.*

FIRST WITCH	Thrice the brinded cat hath mewed.
SECOND WITCH	Thrice and once the hedge-pig whined.
THIRD WITCH	Harpier cries ''Tis time, 'tis time.'
FIRST WITCH	Round about the cauldron go:
	In the poison'd entrails throw.
	Toad, that under cold stone
	Days and nights has thirty one
	Swelter'd venom sleeping got,
	Boil thou first i' the charmed pot.
ALL	Double, double toil and trouble:
	Fire burn and cauldron bubble.
SECOND WITCH	Fillet of a fenny snake,
	In the cauldron boil and bake;
	Eye of newt and toe of frog,
	Wool of bat and tongue of dog,
	Adder's fork and blind-worm's sting,
	Lizard's leg and howlet's wing,
	For a charm of powerful trouble,
	Like a hell-broth boil and bubble.
ALL	Double, double toil and trouble;
	Fire burn and cauldron bubble.
THIRD WITCH	Scale of dragon, tooth of wolf,
	Witches' mummy, maw and gulf
	Of the ravin'd salt-sea shark,
	Root of hemlock digg'd i' the dark,
	Liver of blaspheming Jew,

100

	Gall of goat and slips of yew
	Sliver'd in the moon's eclipse,
	Nose of Turk and Tartar's lips,
	Make the gruel thick and slab:
	Add thereto a tiger's chaudron,
	For the ingredients of our cauldron.
ALL	Double, double toil and trouble:
	Fire burn and cauldron bubble.
SECOND WITCH	Cool it with a baboon's blood,
	Then the charm is firm and good.
SECOND WITCH	By the pricking of my thumbs,
	Something wicked this way comes:
	Open, locks,
	Whoever knocks.
	ENTER MACBETH
MACBETH	How, now, you secret, black, and midnight hags!
	What is't you do?
ALL	A deed without a name.

From *Macbeth* by **William Shakespeare**

Where is the *climax* in that extract?

The Idol

In the following extract, Mafatu, a boy who is terrified of the sea, has left home and has found an island which seems to be uninhabited. Unknown to him, however, the island is used by cannibals. It is their feasting-place. One day, while exploring his new home, Mafatu comes upon a secret spot in the jungle. It is a dark, mysterious area – in the centre of which stands an idol. The boy realises that this is a sacred place of some savage tribe – and to enter is strictly forbidden . . .

The trail led towards the sea, widening as it went. Soon it opened into a cleared circle some hundred feet in circumference. Involuntarily Mafatu started forward, then drew back with a sharp cry. What he beheld filled him with awe and it set him trembling.

He saw a series of wide stone terraces rising in a pyramid many feet high; on top of this pyramid a grotesque idol, hideously ugly, reared in the brilliant sunshine. It was an ancient idol, its contours softened with fungus and lichen, corroded by the rains of ages. The roots of convolvulus writhed about its base. No wind reached this hidden circle, and insects hummed in the hot air. Mafatu felt that he was stifling. His heart pounded. A 'marae' – a Sacred Place.

Scarcely daring to breathe, he advanced a step. Then he drew up short. Around the base of the idol he saw piles of bones, charred but not old. The platform was strewn with them. Bones too large for dogs, too large for pigs. And then Mafatu understood. His heart congealed. This was a 'motu tabu', a Forbidden Island. Here the eaters-of-men made their terrible sacrifices to the Varua Ino!

From *The Boy Who Was Afraid* by **Armstrong Sperry**

You should be very familiar with the word *climax*. On television we see many films and plays – and they must be interesting and exciting in order to encourage people to watch. Notice how quickly each story ends once the climax has been reached.

Of course, it is not only in films and plays that we find climaxes. Our daily lives are, generally, quite uneventful, not like the lives led by television and film heroes and heroines. The lives that they lead on the screen have to be exciting.

We are different. We must live *real* lives, but even so, we have our own little climaxes. They may be such things as parties, prize-winning days, attendances at weddings as bridesmaids, the day we leave school, the start of our working lives, passing important examinations, getting married.

There are scores of other examples, of course. Think of a gardener growing flowers and vegetables to exhibit in an agricultural show. The climax for him comes when his produce is actually on display and being judged.

Take another example, say, a dramatic production. The months of rehearsal are followed by the climax which is the public performance.

You might be an athlete. After weeks or months of training and practising you reach your climax – Sports Day.

In order to reach a climax in anything we climb higher and higher, up 'steps', as it were. Look at these words:

whisper; mutter; speak; shout; yell; roar.

Can you see how the words *climb*; each word being 'stronger', or more intense, than the word before it?

Here is another example:

minute; small; large; enormous.

It is not necessary to write a complete story in order to reach a climax. Even a sentence may have its own high point:

a The people murmured and grew restless until they finally burst out, a screaming mob.

b The sound of footsteps came on – up the stairs, along the landing until they stopped – outside the door.

c Follow your spirit, and upon this charge
Cry 'God for Harry, England and St. George'.

William Shakespeare

d The cloud-capped towers, the gorgeous palaces,
The solemn temples, the great globe itself,
. . . shall dissolve!

William Shakespeare

Dramatic Movement

Individual work

Remember your *senses* and use them. Mime the following:

1 Imagine that you are asleep. Close your eyes and relax.
2 Something wakes you.
3 Wake up s-l-o-w-l-y.
4 Try to establish the origin of the sound.
5 Whatever it is – it comes towards your door. Sit up – horror-stricken.
6 The door opens and . . .
   THIS IS THE CLIMAX
   . . . something enters.

Working in pairs

Imagine that you are performing this for young children.

a One of you is the Princess in the 'Sleeping Beauty'. Number two is the old woman who lived in the tower at the top of the castle. One day the Princess discovers the old woman. The child shows interest in the spinning which the other is doing. Gradually the child's interest grows until she is encouraged to try herself – with drastic results. The *climax* comes when the Princess falls.

b Number one is a spy who is in a house, trying to open a safe which contains secret documents. The atmosphere is tense. Number two – a Government Agent – enters.

Working in groups

a You are people living on an island under the shadow of a volcano which is about to erupt. Work on the island carries on as usual. The open-air market is held. The children go to school. Smaller children play in the streets. Suddenly the climax is reached when the volcano erupts and chaos follows.

b You probably know the story of 'Pandora's Box'. Do you remember the part where the girl and the boy decide to open the forbidden box? When they did so – out flew hideous winged creatures. They were all the troubles that we now have in the world. Perform this story, creating the right atmosphere and rising to a climax.

Style

In your writing you should try to develop a varying and interesting style.

Read the following aloud:

He stood in the shadows. He was near the village hall. It was late last night. He was evil-looking. We did not want him to see us. We hid in a doorway. We stayed until he went away.

There is nothing wrong with any of the sentences in that passage. Using a series of short sentences only, however, generally results in a jerky effect, which does nothing to enhance our composition. The above extract can be improved by combining the sentences:
   e.g. Late last night the evil-looking man stood in the shadows near the village hall. We did not want him to see us, so we hid in a doorway, where we stayed until he went away.

Note *how* the various sentences are joined. By using a variety of joining words, combine the following groups of short sentences to form two or three longer sentences in each case. You may change the order of words if you wish.

a We set out. The sun was shining. There were some clouds in the sky. The wind was cold. We arrived at the park. Large drops of rain began to fall. We returned home.

b Jack went to the library. He chose a book. He returned home. He started to read the book. It was boring. He read a magazine instead.

c The little old man sat in the park. He sat there every day. He was alone. He was not lonely. People passed by. They always spoke to him. He did not like some of the children. They teased him.

d The big car pulled away from the kerb. It was a black car. A boy ran across the road. The driver of the car braked hard. He was unable to stop in time. His vehicle struck the boy. The boy was fortunate. He was not injured.

e We were returning home. It was in the early hours of the morning. We saw a strange object. It was in the sky. It was saucer-shaped. It was surrounded by an orange glow. There was no sound coming from it.

f The train entered the outskirts of the city. John and Mary stood. They collected their luggage. It was in the rack. Sandra remained seated. She had to travel a further hundred miles. It would be a long journey. She would be without her friends. The thought was far from pleasing.

Just as a series of short sentences can irritate a reader, so can a very long, complicated sentence confuse him:
e.g. We met outside the station and, when we were all gathered, we went inside and caught the ten-thirty train which took us to

London where we first visited the Wax-works, spending most of the morning there, before we went to a small, but very pleasant cafe, where we had a good lunch before going on to the Zoo where we spent an enjoyable afternoon.

Rewrite the following sentences, making each long sentence into two, three or even four shorter ones. Make them smooth-flowing, avoiding any jerkiness:

a Bill and Ted decided to explore the old castle which stood amongst trees on top of a hill and which had an eerie look about it, especially on moonlit nights, so that local people said that it was haunted, a ghost having been seen by several citizens, including two clergymen and a magistrate, none of them being men given to 'imagining things'.

b The small cave, which was situated high up on the mountainside, but well below the snow-line, was believed to have been inhabited, two centuries past, by a hermit, but whether or not that was true no one knew, though, certainly it had been occupied during the war by refugees.

c The soldiers arrived just after noon, but it was almost six o'clock before they had pitched all their tents and dug their slit-trenches, and by that time it was dark, so that cooking fires could not be lighted, the enemy being close enough to see the smallest flame.

d The senior pupils were ready to set off on the outing, but the coach had not arrived and Mr Philips, the Headmaster, who was very annoyed, asked his secretary to telephone the company, telling the man in charge that he wished to know the reason for the delay.

e After looking forward for so long to a day at the seaside, Lorraine found it difficult to believe that she and her friends, all of whom were as excited as she was, were actually on their way, but as the miles flashed by they all became impatient, waiting for their first glimpse of the ocean.

f The small dog ran along the beach, splashing through rock-pools and jumping over the smaller boulders, but he failed to notice several sharp pieces of stone and he landed on one of them, hurting his foot, yet even though the injury was not very serious, it caused him to limp for days afterwards.

Generally speaking, a good style of writing requires a variation in the length of the sentences written, a mixture of long and short.

Of course, there *are* times when a series of either long or short sentences may be necessary for the writer to achieve the effect he desires:

e.g. We pushed away from the shore as gently as possible, sliding the oars into the water with scarcely a splash. The merest sound would carry easily across that great expanse and we could not afford to be heard. For a moment the moon appeared, slipping from behind a patch of black cloud and flooding the lake with cold, revealing light. At once David stopped rowing and both he and I held our breaths, not daring to move the tiniest of muscles. Were we even now visible to our enemies, those unseen watchers on the opposite shore?

What kind of effect was the writer trying to achieve in that passage? Has he been successful? If he has – can you explain why?

Now read this passage:

Suddenly Steven was alert. The road ahead was blocked. Quickly he glanced in the mirror. His pursuers were still behind – and gaining on him. What was he to do? Progress forward must end in a matter of seconds. The tree – for that was the object barring his way – was too large for him to move. He stabbed his foot at the brake pedal. Nothing happened. Again he tried. Again it was in vain. Panic seized him. His arms began to shake. His legs trembled. So – this was the end! He wished he knew how to pray.

It was then that he noticed the narrow track. It led off to the right, on his side of the tree. Savagely he pulled on the wheel. He heard the tyres crunch. Earth flew up. Mud spattered the windscreen. The car rocked wildly, but the immediate danger had passed.

Now he had only to worry about the men behind him.

Comment on the style of that passage.

Write the following contrasting paragraphs, using an appropriate style for each:

a (i) Describe a scene at dusk when the fishing-boats are leaving the harbour.
   (ii) Describe the same scene the following morning when the catches have been landed.
b (i) Describe a hot afternoon in the park, and
   (ii) evening at a fun-fair.
c (i) Describe a man digging his garden, and
   (ii) a street accident. (Concentrate on the panic, not on the injuries sustained.)
d (i) Describe a scene at a busy market, and
   (ii) the same scene at the end of the day as the traders pack up and prepare to go home.

e (*i*) Describe a village cricket match on a quiet afternoon, and

(*ii*) an exciting moment at a football match.

f (*i*) Describe a trip on a canal long-boat, and

(*ii*) a scene on a reservoir where various water-sports are being held.

g *i*) Describe a prize-giving ceremony at a school, and

(*ii*) another school activity, such as the annual staff *v*. pupils match.

h (*i*) Describe a scene on a farm during the hay-making season, and

(*ii*) a scene in an industrial town during the home-going rush-hour.

i (*i*) Describe a scene at a circus after a dangerous animal has escaped, and

(*ii*) a scene in the hills where a party is on a walking tour.

j (*i*) Describe a walk on the downs on a very calm day, and

(*ii*) a walk in the town on a very windy day.

You may also add variety to your compositions by using both Direct and Indirect Speech:

e.g. *Direct:* 'It's raining,' said John.

Indirect: John said that it was raining.

In order to change Direct Speech into Indirect Speech the main rules to follow are:

1 Quotation marks are omitted.

2 The verb is written in the *past* tense.

3 First person pronouns become third person pronouns.

Indirect Speech is also known as Reported Speech. Remembering that should help to make conversion easier. If you imagine that you *have been speaking* to someone and you then go to another place and tell someone else what the person *said* – you are *reporting*. As time has *passed* since you saw the original person – then what he said is now in the *past*.

Wherever possible use the word 'that' after the word 'said'. Doing so will make the rest of the sentence form correctly:

e.g. Mary said, 'It's time to go home.'

Mary said *that* it was time to go home.

Questions are a little more difficult to convert to Indirect Speech.

e.g. Jill asked, 'What is the time?'

This may be converted in several ways:

Jill asked the time.

Jill asked what was the time.

Jill asked what the time was.

Jill asked if anyone knew the time.

Rewrite the following as Indirect (Reported) Speech:

a 'We went to the zoo,' said John.

b 'My television set won't work,' said Mrs Weston.

c 'Where is my book?' asked Jane.

d 'The film was boring,' said Jane. 'I didn't like it at all.'

e Jack said, 'We took five photographs before the film ran out.'

f 'What time shall we meet?' asked Kate.

g The policeman said, 'This road is closed. All motorists must make a detour.'

h 'Why are the lights still on?' asked the teacher.

i 'I haven't caught a fish all day,' complained Peter.

j Philip asked John, 'When will you have your new motor-cycle?'

Rewrite the following sentences in Direct Speech:

a Mr Jones said that his shop would remain closed on Saturday.

b Bill asked if anyone had seen the football.

c The maid said that the visitors had arrived.

d Fred asked June if she liked riding horses.

e The milkman asked Mrs Reynolds how many pints she required.

f Nancy complained that she had a severe headache.

g The teacher asked Emma if she had completed her homework.

h The driver asked the children to climb aboard the coach quickly and carefully.

i Ted told his uncle that he was very pleased with his new camera.

j Mr Smith asked if any member of the party could drive a car.

Rewrite this passage, changing the Direct Speech into Indirect (Reported) Speech:

At last the journey was over. 'You can stretch your legs now,' the driver told his passengers. 'Better take advantage of the break to have something to eat.'

'Have we much further to go?' asked one old man. 'It's been a long day.' He looked about him at his companions, as if seeking support in their agreeing with his statement. No one moved. No one spoke. The old man returned his attention to the driver. 'Maybe it hasn't been so long really,' he said quietly.

The driver nodded. 'A cup of tea and a sandwich will soon buck you up,' he said. So saying, he turned and led the way into the small, unpleasant-looking cafe.

Rewrite the following passage, changing Indirect Speech into Direct Speech:

As the three boys entered the field a man in uniform approached and told them that they were trespassing and must leave at once.

Eric, the oldest, stepped forward and pointed out that they had always been allowed to go into the field. He wished to know why they were no longer permitted to do so.

The man turned and pointed to a far corner of the field. There the boys saw other soldiers standing close to an army lorry. All three recognised the vehicle. The man turned back and told them that no one was allowed near the field because an unexploded bomb, left over from the war, had been discovered. He added that the men hoped to make it safe within a few hours.

Eric asked if they would then be able to go into the field. The man said that they would.

Punctuation

Punctuate the following passages:

a are you going to town on wednesday why id like to go with you

b having entered the cave linda was not sure that they had made the right decision it may be the wrong one she whispered jean frowned its a little late to say that now isnt it we can hardly go out again with that man sitting up on that rock for a moment linda made no answer being too interested in a tiny glimmer far ahead she moved on beckoning jean to follow despite the boulders with which the floor of the cave was strewn they made good progress finally linda halted there she pointed what is it asked jean its light linda made no attempt to disguise both her triumph and her impatience with her friend its an opening she explained we can get out so i was right wasnt i

c on tuesday they visited the tower of london where they saw the crown jewels very impressive admitted graham but what about the rest of the week jack consulted the list theres still hyde park the zoo buckingham palace and trafalgar square we should manage them tomorrow or thursday graham nodded sounds all right but im running out of money what about you jack grinned well have to walk home he said still the exercise will do us good

d id like to see the manager said mrs wilson her round face red with anger courtesy costs nothing young man she prodded at the youthful assistant forcing him to take refuge behind a filing-cabinet well yes madam if I might pass the young man now thoroughly terrified nodded towards the door marked

manager heavily the woman turned and then moved her ample
form so that the assistant might obey her original command and
when i make another complaint she said to his retreating back
youd better see to it that im treated with more respect so saying
she folded her arms across her chest and fixed a superior
expression on her face ill never darken the doors of this shop
again she added

If we cannot find enough exciting moments, either in real life or
in literature, we can always create our own by writing them
ourselves:

e.g. The clearing was ahead, no more than a metre from us. A
fringe of tall trees separated us from our goal. I thought back to
the early morning, when we had first left the blazing heat of the
great plain to enter the forest where the cool air struck us, almost
brutally. As we groped our way between the mighty, black trees
we both felt our nerves tightening. Len had said nothing. Neither
had I, but I knew that he felt the same as I did. And now we had
arrived – but what was waiting for us in that clearing? I was in
front and it seemed natural for me to break through the forest
curtain – which I did – and I froze immediately as I found myself
staring at the most horrific-looking monster it was possible to
imagine, if, in fact, it could be imagined.

Now write some paragraphs, trying to end each passage on a high
note (*climax*). Some suggestions are given.

a It is a summer night and you are in bed when it starts to rain.
   You get up and look through the window. Describe how the
   storm grows from a gentle drizzle to a raging thunder-storm.

b A picnic is being enjoyed by a group of friends when an angry
   bull suddenly appears in the field.

c An aeroplane full of passengers is flying over the Atlantic
   Ocean when fire breaks out.

d One day you decide to explore the ruins of a castle which is near
   your home.

e Some friends are at an open-air dog-show when the weather
   suddenly changes.

f An explorer in the jungle has injured his foot and is lying in a
   clearing when some warriors of an unknown tribe appear.

g You are trapped in a lift which has stopped between floors.

h You have been left in charge of the house one day. It is now
   nearing the time when your parents are due back and you have
   not done the housework. Nor have you got a meal ready. In
   your hurry you find that nothing seems to go right.

i Look at the photograph and then compose any piece of writing that it suggests to you:

Dialogue

If you go to the theatre you will notice that there is usually one, if not more, interval between the acts. You will also notice that the story of the play rises to reach a climax just before each interval. Can you suggest any reason for this?

Let us have a look at a play – the part just before the first interval. That is, the part which leads up to a climax.

The scene is the interior of a lonely cottage one Christmas Eve. Outside the wind is chill, and the ground is gripped by a hard frost. All is covered with a thick layer of snow.

At the moment when we enter the cottage we discover a Mother and two children sitting near the fire. The Mother has been telling the children a story concerning the Ice Fairy who visits people on Christmas Eve. The people she chooses to visit have suffered a grievous loss during the year which has just passed. It is said that when she is about to enter a house strange whistling noises are heard – whistlings more piercing and louder than those of the wind:

JOHN But, Mother – the Ice Fairy – she won't visit us. We haven't had . . .

MOTHER A tragedy?

JOHN Yes.

MOTHER Until last summer we were happy. And then . . .

MARY Be quiet, John. You'll upset her.

MOTHER No! It's all right, Mary. I feel fine now. It's just that since your father died things haven't been too easy.

JOHN I'm sorry, Mother. I didn't mean to make you sad.

(There is a pause)

MOTHER Come along. It's time you children had supper.

MARY (Moving towards the cupboard)

If only she'd visit us!

MOTHER The Ice Fairy?

(She laughs)

Don't wish too hard. She might come if you do.

JOHN (Excitedly)

If only she would.

MOTHER (Suddenly serious)

Don't be too eager. She doesn't always bring *good* luck.

MARY (Also serious)

What do you mean?

MOTHER They say that sometimes . . .

JOHN Yes! Go on, Mother.

MOTHER Perhaps not. Come on. Supper!

MARY Please, Mother – *do* tell us.

(There is another pause)

MOTHER Well – it may only be a story. They say that sometimes – instead of bringing good luck – sometimes . . . she takes one of the family away. And that person is never seen again.

(The children are horror-struck)

JOHN What if . . . what if she comes here?

MARY No – don't say that, John!

(The noise of the wind grows louder)

What was that?

MOTHER Only the wind

(JOHN moves to the window and listens)

JOHN Sh!

(They all listen. Suddenly – above the wind they hear a piercing whistle)

MOTHER (Putting the children behind her)

No! No! It can't be!

(The whistling grows louder and comes nearer. The room grows darker)

MARY It's her!

(She screams)

It's her!

MOTHER Hush, children.

JOHN She takes one of the family . . . and they never see . . .

(The whistling becomes almost deafening – and then stops suddenly. There is a brief silence, and then the door begins to open . . . as the curtain falls.)

Now read this piece of dialogue aloud:

JILL I'll be going into town this afternoon. Like to come with me?

MARY I would. It won't cost much, will it?

JILL Not a lot. Anyway, I'll pay.

MARY We'll go to the Sales while we're there, shall we?

JILL Oh, I don't know about that. Mum says there's no such thing as a bargain.

MARY My mum says the same, but she'll go if she's given a chance.

Notice that the use of contracted forms (i.e. I'll; won't; we'll; we're; there's; she'll; she's.) make the conversation sound realistic. In your other writing you should use the complete words (i.e. I shall; will not; we shall etc.)

Write pieces of interesting dialogue, rising to a climax in each case:

a Imagine that you and a friend are unpacking Christmas presents. Each parcel reveals something which is more exciting than the last – until the 'special' gift is opened.

b You and a friend are waiting to see some famous person pass by in procession. Write the conversation that might lead up to her/his actual appearance.

c Imagine that you are waiting for the results of a very important examination to be posted on the school noticeboard. Write the conversation which might take place between the two of you while you wait.

d You have just taken part in some competitive event (such as a skating contest; a horse-riding competition; a race; a gymnastic display etc.) and you are waiting for the judges' decisions. Write the conversation that might take place between you and another competitor.

e Two of you have just attended an interview for a post. While you are waiting for the committee to decide on the appointment you talk to another candidate.

Look at the sketch-map of the island on p. 114.

a You have been cast up on the island. Describe how you arrived there – and why.

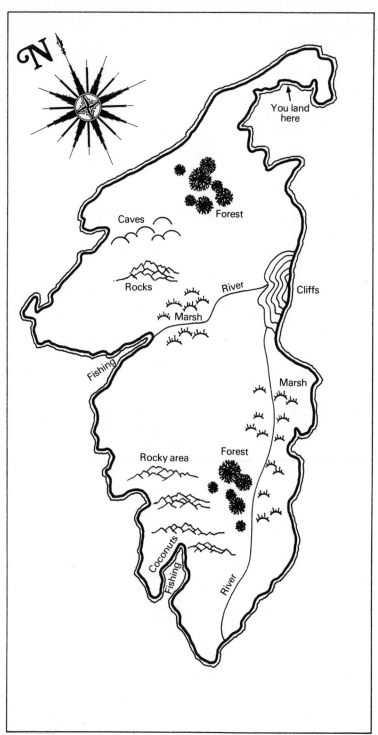

The Island

b Describe how you spent your first night alone.

c Describe your first tour of discovery.

d Explain where you make your 'permanent' camp, and describe its construction.

e Explain how you made your way from the north of the island to the coconut grove in the south, crossing a fast-flowing river at least once on the way.

f Describe contingency plans made by you in case rescue will be possible.

g Describe how you found food, there being no animals on the island.

h Write a diary for a week, giving information about your life on the island after you had 'settled in'.

i Describe your eventual rescue. Try to explain your feelings at the time.

Diaries

Write a diary for a week for each of the following people, making the last entry in each case the climax:

a Imagine that you are to be chief bridesmaid at an important wedding. The whole week is one of preparation and growing excitement.

b You are to take part in a tournament of some kind (such as a cycling race; a canoe race; a musical competition etc.) Write your diary for a week, finishing on the evening of the day of the actual event.

c Imagine that you are a famous explorer. Write your diary, ending with your making some great discovery. It might be a good idea to look up information before attempting this, and the next, piece of work.

d Do the same as you did in (c), but imagine that you are a great scientist or inventor.

e You are taking part in a dramatic production, either as an actor/actress or as the producer. Write your diary for a week, ending after the actual performance.

Write diaries for a week for each of the following, making them as interesting and as informative as possible:

a a light-house keeper.

b a canal lock-keeper's wife.

c a country policeman.

d the manager of a garage.

e the proprietor of a shop.
f a kennel-maid.
g an usherette at a theatre.
h a village post-master/mistress.
i the curator of a museum.
j a street-corner newspaper-seller.
k someone on a cycling holiday
l a newspaper photographer.
m a health visitor.
n a telephone engineer.
o a factory worker.
p a school caretaker.
q a librarian.
r the groundsman in a large park.
s a member of a school field-course.
t a chauffeur.

Magazine Articles

The following might appear in a school magazine:

A Helping Hand

Twenty members of the Fourth Year have enjoyed a very rewarding term, thanks to their 'Helping Hand' project, organised by Mr Lewis, Head of General Studies. During the Christmas Term Mr Lewis asked for volunteers to take part in what he called 'Community Help'. About thirty of us went along. Some were not interested in what we were told about helping old people in the neighbourhood, during and after school hours, but twenty of us stayed.

Since then, throughout the Easter Term, we have gone out twice a week, on Tuesdays and Thursdays, to give a 'helping hand' where needed.

First, we were divided into small groups of two, three or four – according to the jobs to be done. The big groups mainly did gardening. Some of the girls just visited and talked with lonely old ladies. Jennifer Scott from 4R and June Maynard from 4K said that the times spent talking to their particular old ladies have been some of the most interesting moments of their lives.

Jim Talbot and I were 'assigned' to Mr Evans, a ninety-year-old man who has lived alone for eighteen years. None of his family – he says he has four sons and one daughter – ever go near him. The job he most wanted us to do was to clear out his attic. He, himself, has not been upstairs for eight years. The attic was in a very bad state. Everything was covered by thick dust and there were cobwebs, like ropes, hanging everywhere. Mr Evans asked us to take all the stuff down-stairs. We did – and it took us three weeks to do it. He told us interesting stories about some of the items he had kept – bits and pieces from the First World War, old school books – all sorts of things.

Billy Smith, Jack Lewis and Ted Phelps from 4R transformed a disabled pensioner's garden from a 'jungle' to a 'park'. That was how the old man described it. The strange thing is – Billy, Jack and Ted all *hate* gardening, but they said that they really enjoyed the exercise.

The 'Helping Hand' scheme has been judged a success by all of us who took part, but – more important – by all those who received help. They have told Mr Lewis that they hope the visits will continue. Mr Lewis is prepared to carry on – and so are we.

M. Thompson 4B

A magazine article like that should give facts that are presented in a readable manner. Now see what you can do:

a Write an article for a school magazine in which you describe an interest that you have outside the school. (For instance, horseriding; dancing classes; gymnastic club etc.)

b Imagine that you are the Secretary of a school club. (For example, tennis; cricket; hiking; chess; stamp-collecting etc.) Write the annual report in which you outline the year's work in the club, paying particular attention to the highlight of the season.

c Write a magazine article in which you describe some exciting incident that you have experienced.

d Imagine that you are the Headteacher of your school. Write your report for the magazine, describing the year's outstanding event.

e Imagine that you are writing a magazine article at the end of your first year in the secondary school.

Compose any piece of writing that is suggested to you by this photograph:

Stories

Write stories suggested by the following, ending each one on a high note – a climax:

a You have decided to do one good deed every day. One evening you realise that you have not done so that day and you make up your mind to do so at once.

b 'At last they set off, though John was a little anxious about the brakes on his bicycle . . .

c A boy/girl living in medieval Britain is involved in a capture and an escape.

d 'Tom knew that the lock of the cage was faulty . . .

e One night you catch the last 'bus home, thinking that the vehicle is full of 'ordinary' people. You are wrong . . .

f Imagine that you are a small child going to school for the first time.

g 'Scare.'

h Write about an important moment in the life of a famous doctor.

i 'Everything would have been all right if it had not rained . . .

j Birthday presents are being opened. One strange-shaped parcel bears an even stranger stamp.

Compose any pieces of writing that these quotations suggest to you:

a And ice, mast-high, came floating by,
   As green as emerald.
   S. T. Coleridge

b Save that from yonder ivy-mantled tower
   The moping owl does to the moon complain.
   Thomas Gray

c One of the pleasantest things in the world is going on a trip; but I like to go by myself.
   William Hazlitt

d A traveller, by the faithful hound,
   Half-buried in the snow was found.
   H. W. Longfellow

e 'Three years,' I cried. 'Were you shipwrecked?'
   'Nay, mate,' said he – 'marooned.'
   R. L. Stevenson

Reports

Write these newspaper reports, ending each one with a climax:
a Information has been received that strange visitors will land on

a deserted beach. You hide amongst the rocks and wait.

b An unidentified object has been found on a demolition site.

c A visit to a circus. The most exciting act.

d An old railway-bridge is to be blown up by demolition experts.

e An unexpected event occurs in the main ring at an agricultural show.

f A barbecue and a firework display form the climax to a summer fete.

g An air show; a motor show; an exhibition of homes and buildings; a fashion show; an antique fair; a steam fair; any other sort of display or exhibition.

6 SUMMARISING

We have all met the person who, in answer to our question 'What was the film about?' treats us to a long, involved description which includes the most minute of details. What we *really* wanted was a brief summary of the plot of the film and, perhaps, an even briefer opinion of it.

Producing an adequate summary of a passage of English, or of a report, for example, can be quite difficult. Pupils in school frequently encounter problems in this area for two *main* reasons:

1 They are unable to decide what is important information in the original passage and which must be included in the summary.
2 Their vocabularies are weak so that they are not able to use one word in place of several.

> e.g. Jack was a *man who was* keen *on ringing church bells.*
> Jack was a keen *campanologist.*

Vocabulary practice

Summarise the following sentences by using *one word* in each to replace those underlined.

a During the war vehicles were used which were able to move both on land and on water.
b The old man died a pauper because he was a person who gave his money to various charities.
c Jim's ambition was to be able to speak and write several languages.
d The man who was in charge of the museum met the school party and acted as their guide on a conducted tour.
e The boys explored the old cottage which was deserted and in a state of near-ruin.
f Mark went to the seaside where he recovered after his recent illness.
g Barbara was finally sent to a doctor who carried out operations.
h Mr Williams was worried because his wife was a person who walked in her sleep.
i On the first day of term the teacher dictated the times and places of the week's lessons.
j The man who trapped rabbits and pheasants illegally was caught by the game-keeper.

k Philip was frequently in trouble at school because his writing was so <u>poorly formed</u> that no one could read it.

l The Captain lowered the sails because he realised that a storm <u>was about to break</u> at any moment.

m Many people who lived during the reign of Queen Elizabeth I were <u>unable to read or write.</u>

n Pauline and Stewart made an appointment to see a <u>man whose work was concerned with drawing up plans for houses and other buildings.</u>

o Mr Jones grew flowers in his front garden, and <u>cabbage, onions, parsnips, beans and peas</u> in the back.

p All doctors have to study <u>the structure of the human body</u> before they can qualify.

q Disasters often occur when <u>mountains that throw out molten lava</u> erupt.

r Many people study <u>the stars and the movements of the planets.</u>

s Eric owns a shop where he sells <u>various pieces of furniture that were manufactured several hundred years ago.</u>

t David has the responsible job of <u>planning and guiding the route taken by the aeroplane.</u>

Summarising fiction

Read this fable:

It happened that the Wind and the Sun became involved in an argument. 'I am much stronger than you are,' boasted the Wind. Of course, the Sun disagreed. The only way to resolve the dispute, they decided, was by means of a contest.

'But what kind of competition?' asked the Sun.

For a moment the Wind pondered. Then, looking down, he saw a lonely traveller making his way across a great stretch of open moorland. The man moved slowly, his journey being hindered by the heavy box which he carried under his thick, flowing cloak.

'We'll use him,' said the Wind.

'How?' asked the Sun. 'He is a mere traveller. He cannot prove which of us is the stronger.'

'His cloak!' answered the Wind. 'We shall see which of us will be the first to make him remove it!'

The Sun agreed and the contest began. The Wind blew fiercely, hoping to tear the cloak away from the traveller, but the harder he blew the tighter the man wrapped the garment about himself. At last the Wind blew himself out and gave up the struggle.

Then the Sun shone, spreading his warm beams across the stretch of moorland. For a while the man continued walking, but as he grew hotter and hotter he became more and more exhausted. Finally, in order to cool himself, he was forced to take off his cloak, thus making the Sun the winner of the competition.

(239 words)

Suppose you were asked to summarise that story in about one third of its original length. How do you start?

1 Pick out the essential points and write them down in note form.
2 Check that you have included all relevant material.
3 Write out the main points as a continuous, flowing passage. Do *not* include Direct Speech in your final version.

e.g. *Main points*

1 Wind and Sun quarrel. Who is the stronger?
2 They decide to hold a contest.
3 Who will be the first to compel a traveller to remove his cloak?
4 Wind blew hard, trying to tear away cloak, but failed.
5 Sun shone. Heat too much for traveller who removed cloak.

Final version

In order to decide which of them was the stronger the Wind and the Sun decided to hold a contest. Which of them would be the first to cause a traveller to remove his cloak? The Wind blew fiercely, hoping to tear away the cloak, but he was unsuccessful. Then the Sun shone, heating the traveller to such a degree that he quickly removed his cloak.

(66 words)

Summarising facts

Read the following passage and then make a summary of it in about seventy words:

Andrew Carnegie, who died in 1919, is remembered by most people as a man who did a great deal to help his fellow humans. Although he used his money in many ways, his best known works may be seen in the many hundreds of Libraries that he built throughout this country. In this way he provided people with a means of bettering themselves if they so wished.

During his lifetime he made a vast fortune, but he had not always enjoyed times that were blessed by riches. He was born in Scotland in 1835, and he lived there until he and his family went to set up home in America. Andrew was still a young boy at the time.

In his new home he became a messenger boy whose job it was to deliver telegrams. Later he learned to be an actual operator. As a result of hard and conscientious work he became a superintendant in the company. Such a position, of course, brought with it financial rewards which made it possible for him to invest in land. As that land contained the very valuable commodity of oil he was able to amass even more money.

When he finally retired Andrew Carnegie was an extremely wealthy man, owning many millions of pounds.

MAIN POINTS

Andrew Carnegie. Died 1919.
Philanthropist.
Founded Libraries.
Was not always rich.
Born in Scotland, 1835.
Emigrated to America.
Worked as a messenger boy.
Learned to be an operator.
Became company superintendant.
Amassed money.

FINAL VERSION

Andrew Carnegie, who died in 1919, was a philanthropist who founded hundreds of Libraries throughout the country. Although he amassed a huge fortune, he was not always wealthy. Born in Scotland in 1835, he emigrated to America with his parents. There he worked as a telegraph messenger and then as an operator. Perseverance took him to the rank of company superintendant and brought financial rewards which enabled him to invest in land and oil.

(74 words)

Note: When making a summary, figurative language should be omitted. Lists should be replaced by collective words wherever possible.

Read the following passages and make summaries of them. The number of words stated at the end of each extract is meant to be a guide only.

a The word 'chivalry' frequently brings to mind medieval times, and knights in shining armour riding about the countryside, battling to save damsels in distress. Many exciting stories about such colourful characters have been written, but to be a knight required a man to live to a strict code of behaviour. For example, he was taught that he must never attack an unarmed foe. He was never to perform a dishonourable act, and he should never boast of his victories.

A man could become a knight in one of two ways. The sovereign might 'dub him a knight' by tapping him lightly on the shoulder with a sword. Or he could serve an apprenticeship. Such a route to knighthood began at a very early age, at about seven or eight years, when a boy entered a large household as a page. Learning good manners was an essential part of his training. He was also expected to master some kind of musical instrument and to sing.

After he had served as a page for six or seven years he became a squire, which meant that he was a servant to an established knight. As such he had various duties to perform. Firstly he was expected to care for his master, to tend to his wounds if necessary, to help him put on his armour, to be responsible for conditions of his horse and weapons. He also supported the knight in battle, fighting by his side. In order that he be proficient in his use of arms he had to practise regularly, learning to handle weapons such as the sword, battle-axe and lance.

(100–120 words)

b Wuthering Heights is the name of Heathcliff's dwelling. 'Wuthering' being a significant provincial adjective, descriptive of the atmospheric tumult to which its station is exposed in stormy weather. Pure, bracing ventilation they must have up there at all times, indeed: one may guess the power of the north wind blowing over the edge, by the excessive slant of a few stunted firs at the end of the house; and by a range of gaunt thorns all stretching their limbs one way, as if craving alms of the sun. Happily, the architect had foresight to build it strong: the narrow windows are deeply set in the walls, and the corners defended with large jutting stones.

Before passing the threshold, I paused to admire a quantity of grotesque carving lavished over the front, and specially about the principal door, above which, among a wilderness of crumbling griffins and shameless little boys, I detected the date '1500', and the name 'Hareton Earnshaw'.

One step brought us into the family sitting-room, without any introductory lobby or passage: they call it here 'the house' pre-eminently. It includes kitchen and parlour, generally; but I believe at Wuthering Heights the kitchen is forced to retreat altogether into another quarter: I observed no signs of roasting, boiling, or baking, about the huge fireplace; nor any glitter of copper saucepans and tin cullenders on the walls. One end, indeed, reflected splendidly both light and heat from the ranks of immense pewter pots, interspersed with silver jugs and tankards, towering row after row, on a vast dresser, to the very roof. In an arch under the dresser, reposed a huge, liver-coloured bitch pointer, surrounded by a swarm of squealing puppies; and other dogs haunted other recesses.

From *Wuthering Heights* by **Emily Brontë** (80–90 words)

c Not so long ago it would have been difficult to pick up a newspaper or a magazine without seeing some item about skateboarding, the craze that captured the imaginations of thousands of people, not all of them juveniles. Perhaps the peak of its popularity has been reached, but nothing comparable in favour has yet replaced it.

Forty years ago the school year was measured by a variety of crazes, one succeeding another. A favourite winter pastime was the bowling of hoops. These were large iron rings which were beaten along the roads by means of a stick or a short metal bar. Pupils arriving at school on cold mornings were well-heated, despite a frequent lack of adequate clothing.

Thrashing triangular-shaped wooden tops with a length of string attached to a stick was another popular winter hobby. Householders along the path of the flailing children failed to agree, the cost of replacing windows being high.

Summer days encouraged gentler pastimes, such as marbles, and a game involving cigarette-cards. Here the player flicked the cards against a convenient wall, usually that of the outside lavatories. A card falling on top of another card or cards allowed the thrower to scoop the pool.

(60–80 words)

d A hungry dog, seeing a butcher's shop unattended, crept inside and stole a joint of meat. 'I'll take this deep into the forest,' he said to himself. 'There I can eat it without being disturbed by anyone.'

Happily he trotted along the road out of the town and into the lane that led to the wood. He was certainly going to enjoy his feast.

Very soon he left the lane and took to a narrow path. As he headed for the tall trees he paused to rest for a moment on a bridge. Glancing down into the cool, clear water, he saw his own reflection. He thought that the image was, indeed, another dog, but what really interested him was the fact that it held a large piece of meat in its mouth.

'I'll have that meat!' he snapped.

As he opened his mouth to snatch the prize, his own intended meal fell into the water and sank out of sight.

A fable from Aesop (50–70 words)

e Day after day, month after month, road accidents are reported by the media with sickening regularity, causing us to raise our hands in horror and demand that 'something should be done about it all'. Yet, strangely, accidents in the home, where they occur far more frequently than anywhere else, rarely make news.

Kitchens, it would seem, are often designed to cause damage to the unwary. Liquids boiling in unguarded saucepans are ever a source of temptation to the young child, while bubbling jam-tarts taken from low-level ovens are quite irresistible.

High-level cupboard doors swinging open have tested the sharpness of their metal corners on many a delicate head.

The lounge, of course, presents its own pitfalls, the most notable being an unfenced fire-place. Massive windows and patio-doors are there for the careless to walk through.

The real villain of a house, according to some experts, is the stairs, where frayed carpets, loose rods, and abandoned toys have all taken their toll, especially when the handrail is missing.

One would imagine that a bedroom would be a safe haven. Even there, however, we find the inevitable electric sockets, frayed wires, and worn carpets. And who has not stubbed a toe on the vicious leg of a harmless bed?

(70–90 words)

f At a small distance from the house my predecessor had made a seat overshadowed by a hedge of hawthorn and honeysuckle. Here, when the weather was fine and our labour soon finished, we usually sat together to enjoy an extensive landscape, in the calm of the evening. Here, too, we drank tea, which now was become an occasional banquet; and as we had it but seldom, it diffused a new joy, the preparation for it being made with no small share of bustle and ceremony. On these occasions our two little ones always read for us, and they were regularly served after we had done. Sometimes, to give a variety to our amusements, the girls sung to the guitar; and while they thus formed a little concert, my wife and I would stroll down the sloping field, that was embellished with blue-bells and centaury, talk of our children with rapture, and enjoy the breeze that wafted both health and harmony.

In this manner we began to find that every situation in life may bring its own peculiar pleasures: every morning waked us to a repetition of toil, but the evening repaid it with vacant hilarity.

It was about the beginning of autumn, on a holiday – for I kept such as intervals of relaxation from labour – that I had drawn out my family to our usual place of amusement, and our young musicians began their usual concert. As we were thus engaged, we saw a stag bound nimbly by, within about twenty paces of where we were sitting, and by its panting it seemed pressed by the hunters.

From *The Vicar of Wakefield* by **Oliver Goldsmith** (70–90 words)

g To us today the weather is a constant and favourite topic of conversation, especially in the months of July and August when we are thinking of holidays. Then farmers, too, watch the sky anxiously, praying for perfect hay-making conditions.

To our prehistoric ancestors the weather was much more than a reason for complaining or forecasting. Knowing nothing of damp-courses, loft and wall insulation and central-heating, their homes, being at best caves, were anything but cosy. Their clothing, if they possessed any, was hardly adequate to withstand severe weather.

Consequently they were grateful when the sun seemed to be in constant attendance when summer arrived again. Long hot days brought them warmth and comfort, while extra hours of daylight enabled them to find food more easily. It is not difficult, therefore, for us to understand why they came to look upon the sun as a powerful and, at times, a friendly being.

During grey winter days, when he was chilled by frost, soaked by rain and cut by biting winds, early man probably believed that the sun had deserted him. Naturally he must have asked himself why it should be so. He must have displeased the sun in some way. If, indeed, he had offended the great light in the sky – how was he to encourage it to return?

It seemed that the best answer to such a problem was to offer up some most valuable possession – and *the* most valuable was food. This idea presented another problem. How was such a gift to be delivered? The answer was simple. They burned an animal and allowed the smoke to lift the sacrifice upward to the sun.

(80–100 words)

h There was a certain island in the sea, the only inhabitants of which were an old man, whose name was Prospero, and his daughter Miranda, a very beautiful young lady. She came to this island so young that she had no memory of having seen any other human face than her father's.

They lived in a cave or cell made out of a rock; it was divided into several apartments, one of which Prospero called his study; there he kept his books, which chiefly treated of magic, a study at that time much affected by all learned men; and the knowledge of this art he found very useful to him, for being thrown by a strange chance upon this island, which had been enchanted by a witch called Sycorax, who died there a short time before his arrival, Prospero, by virtue of his art, released many good spirits that Sycorax had imprisoned in the bodies of large trees, because they had refused to execute her wicked command. These gentle spirits were ever after obedient to the will of Prospero. Of these Ariel was the chief.

The lively little sprite Ariel had nothing mischievous in his nature, except that he took rather too much pleasure in tormenting an ugly monster called Caliban, for he owed him a grudge because he was the son of his old enemy Sycorax. This Caliban Prospero found in the woods a strange mishapen thing, far less human in form than an ape.

From *Tales From Shakespeare* by **Charles and Mary Lamb**

(80–100 words)

i A visit to a modern theatre, if no longer regarded as 'an occasion', can be a pleasant experience. Certainly such places of entertainment offer their patrons warmth, comfort, and a clear view of the stage – even if the performances themselves are sometimes second-rate.

Not so fortunate were our predecessors, the first Elizabethans, who were prepared to endure considerable discomfort in order to enjoy the plays. For example, there was no stage-lighting in the public theatres, which meant that such buildings had to be without roofing so that daylight might enter. Unfortunately it frequently rained, even in those days, though we have no evidence to suggest that audiences allowed their spirits to be too depressed by the elements.

The large stage, which projected well into the auditorium, permitted many of the spectators to stand on three sides of it. In consequence they were usually known as the 'groundlings'.

There were no such refinements as curtains that could be closed between actors and audience. Scenery was rarely, if ever, used, but stage properties were employed where necessary. Tables and benches and, perhaps, a sign, were sufficient to suggest that a scene was supposed to be taking place in a tavern. Potted shrubs depicted a forest scene, while a single bed transformed a bare platform into a lady's chamber.

The theatres were not *completely* roofless. Balconies ran around the sides of the building, the top one being sheltered by a narrow rim of thatch. Crude benches were placed in these galleries, and patrons who could afford more than the one penny entrance fee paid by the groundlings watched the performance from the comparative luxury of a sitting position.

Young men-about-town demanded more than a rough plank. They paid the highest entry fee which gave them the privilege of sitting on hired stools that were actually placed on the edge of the stage.

(90–100 words)

j Although Mr Crackit spoke in a scarcely audible whisper, and laughed without noise, Sikes imperiously commanded him to be silent and to get to work. Toby complied, by first producing his lantern, and placing it on the ground; and then by planting himself firmly with his head against the wall beneath the window, and his hands upon his knees, so as to make a step of his back. This was no sooner done than Sikes, mounting upon him, put Oliver gently through the window with his feet first, and, leaving hold of his collar, planted him safely on the floor inside.

'Take this lantern,' said Sikes, looking into the room. 'You see the stairs afore you?'

Oliver, more dead than alive, gasped out, 'Yes.' Sikes, pointing to the street door with the pistol-barrel, briefly advised him to take note that he was within shot all the way, and that if he faltered, he would fall dead that instant.

'It's done in a minute,' said Sikes, in the same low whisper. 'Directly I leave go of you, do your work. Hark!'

'What's that?' whispered the other man.

'Nothing,' said Sikes, releasing the hold of Oliver. 'Now.'

In the short time that he had to collect his senses the boy had firmly resolved that, whether he died in the attempt or not, he would make one attempt to dart upstairs from the hall and alarm the family. Filled with this idea, he advanced at once, but stealthily.

'Come back!' suddenly cried Sikes aloud. 'Back! Back!'

Scared by the sudden breaking of the dead stillness of the place, and by a loud cry which followed it, Oliver let his lantern fall, and knew not whether to advance or fly.

The cry was repeated – a light appeared – a vision of two terrified, half-dressed men at the top of the stairs swam before his eyes – a flash – a loud noise – a smoke – a crash somewhere, but where, he knew not – and he staggered back –

Sikes had disappeared for an instant; but he was up again, and had him by the collar before the smoke had cleared away. He fired his own pistol after the men, who were already retreating, and dragged the boy up. 'Clasp your arm tighter,' said Sikes, as he drew him through the window. 'Give me a shawl here. They've hit him. Quick! Damnation, how the boy bleeds.'

Then came the loud ringing of a bell, mingled with the noise of fire-arms, and the shouts of men, and the sensation of being carried over uneven ground at a rapid pace. And then the noises grew confused in the distance, and a cold deadly feeling crept over the boy's heart; and he saw or heard no more.

From *Oliver Twist* by **Charles Dickens** (120–140 words)

7 PUTTING IT TOGETHER

Throughout this book you have been encouraged to write creatively, and it has been suggested that you emphasise certain aspects. From here on you should write *freely and creatively*, using the skills that you have already practised to write about people, places, things seen and heard – and taking your readers to a climax.

This book is written in English – in the English Language. When you read it with your eyes – your brains turn the words into *meaning* for you.

Whenever you have a thought you have to clothe it in language before you can express it. That is – if you wish to communicate your thoughts and feelings to someone else you must either write or speak. Thus you express yourself.

A Tale To Tell

Suppose you woke up one morning and discovered that all the television sets, cinemas, dance-halls, swimming-pools, theatres ... and all other places of entertainment ... had vanished. Would your life be any different from what it is now? What would you do in the evenings, for example? You would probably be bored in no time.

Many years ago people had none of these ways of passing time. So they had to make up their own entertainments. In the summer this was fairly easy. They might enjoy gatherings on the village green, for instance. Occasionally a fair was held. There were wrestling and boxing matches sometimes.

The winter, however, was different. Frequently the cold dark nights kept people indoors. There was not even gas or electric lighting then. How, then, did they entertain themselves?

They used one of the oldest forms of diversion – story-telling. Usually in a family the father or the mother had a store of tales which had been handed down from their parents who had, in turn, heard them from *their* parents. Such stories were called 'Folk Tales'.

Not only were there family story-tellers. There were, too, the wandering tellers of tales. Generally these men were minstrels. They carried stringed musical instruments and often told their tales in song. It has been said that such people were our earliest 'newspapers' in that they carried the 'news' from place to place.

Today – in some parts of the world – there are probably still wandering story-tellers – especially in lonely villages where few people can read and write.

Of course, you *can* read and write, but when you were very small you loved someone to 'tell you a story'. Then the day came when you began to 'read' stories for yourselves, usually picture stories, and you made up the words. Later, at the age of six or seven, you found that you could read real stories.

Now you have stories in many forms, such as 'reading' stories, danced stories (ballet), acted stories (plays), filmed stories, sung stories (opera and musical plays), picture stories and so on. Some of these you like and some you might dislike, but it is certain that you like some form of story. You *do* realise, of course, that all the films and plays you see *are* stories – and that all had to be written down before they could be filmed or performed.

Probably the first stories that you can remember having been told are nursery rhymes – which *are stories*. Then came Fairy Tales. Of course, you are much too old for fairy tales now. Or are you? Did you go to the pantomime last year? What did you see? 'Little Red Riding Hood'? 'Jack the Giant-killer'? 'Cinderella'? 'Jack and the Beanstalk'? 'Mother Goose'? 'Snow White'?

Old fairy tales are very much like our modern stories really. What do you find in them? Look at an example, say, *Snow White*.

1 We have a hero(es) .... The Prince. (The Dwarfs)
2 We have a heroine .... Snow White.
3 We have a villain .... The Wicked Queen.

What about *Little Red Riding Hood*?

1 We have a heroine .... Red Riding Hood.
2 We have a hero .... The Woodcutter.
3 We have a villain .... The Wolf.

There there is *Cinderella*.

1 We have a heroine .... Cinderella.
2 We have a hero .... The Prince.
3 We have a villain (two). .... The Ugly Sisters.

As you see, all these stories have the same basic ingredients.

What about a modern story, say, on television? All the cowboy films have heroes, heroines and villains. So do all the crime thrillers. Then there are the stories about doctors and hospitals. Can you suggest an unusual type of 'villain' that might be found in such stories?

When you watch a thrilling programme on television you will notice that if there is an interval it usually comes at an exciting moment – at the moment when tension has been built up to a high pitch . . . that is . . . when the *suspense* is at its highest point. Every good story requires some kind of suspense, even love stories. For example, you are kept wondering 'Will he ask her to marry him?' If he does – will she say 'Yes'? And if she does – will they live happily ever after? In programmes with a hospital background, for example, there is usually a good deal of suspense. Have you noticed how you sit almost breathlessly when you see 'surgeons' performing some dangerous 'operation'? In cowboy stories (Westerns) you know that the hero will win in the end, but he has to face a great deal of danger before he does so. Here we have suspense.

Even your own life has its moments of suspense. 'Will I pass the examination?' 'Will my parents allow me to go to the party on Saturday?' 'Will I be chosen as captain of the team?'

Compose any piece of writing that this photograph suggests to you. For example, you might write a story, a poem, a letter, a report, a description etc.

Dramatic Movement

Let us start by taking some of the simplest stories known to us –
nursery rhymes. Naturally, you are too old for such tales now –
but you are not going to perform them as they are told.

> e.g. Little Miss Muffet
> Sat on a tuffet,
> Eating her curds and whey.
> Along came a spider
> And sat down beside her,
> And frightened Miss Muffet away.

a Mime this story first.
b Now try to add some words of your own.
   This is all rather tame, isn't it?
c Try again, but this time bring the story up to date.
   Work in pairs:
   For example, Number 1 (Miss Muffet) sits at home, busy at
   some work (sewing, reading, doing housework). Number 2
   (The Spider), is now some 'unearthly being/creature'. Enter
   and frighten Number 1. Really act this scene and try to create
   some 'atmosphere'.
d Now see what you can do with 'Jack and Jill'. Perform this in
   pairs – first as the original story suggests.
     Now bring it up to date.
     E.g. Number 1 (Jack) and Number 2 (Jill) are two soldiers
   who have to break into an enemy camp in order to steal some
   secret documents. That is, they have to make an effort – just as
   the original Jack and Jill made an effort to climb a hill and draw
   some water from a well.
     Having made their effort – what happens next? Danger?
   Well – what about disturbing the two soldiers while they are
   busy at the safe, or as they are about to make their escape?
e Having had some practice, see what you can do with other
   nursery rhymes. You should be able to bring them up to date if
   you use some imagination. Here are some suggestions:
   Little Jack Horner.   Old King Cole.
   Hickory Dickory Dock.   Wee Willie Winkie.
   Sing a Song of Sixpence.
f So much for nursery rhymes. Let us move on to other old
   favourites. (At least – they were favourites with you once.)
   These stories provide many opportunities for acting: e.g.
     There are Kings and Queens, requiring majestic, proud
   performances.

There are 'Little People', requiring light, airy movements.
There are Witches – cunning, frightening creatures.

Here are some suggestions:

Goldilocks and the Three Bears.
Red Riding Hood.
Snow White.
The Twelve Dancing Princesses.
Beauty and the Beast.
Cinderella.
The Goose Girl.

Remember – you do not have to perform these as the original stories suggest. There is plenty of room here for you to use real initiative in modernising the tales.

Now see if you can create some *suspense*. As your teacher describes the scene, perform the actions, trying to imagine yourself *really there*.

You are sitting alone in the house. It is midnight and you are enjoying a thrilling book. All is very still. Then, suddenly, you think that you hear a creak on the stairs.

You are nervous. You stop reading and *listen*.

All is quiet again and you continue reading.

There is the creak again – louder. You *move* cautiously to the door which leads to the stairs. *Listen* again.

You take hold of the handle of the door.

Will you open it? What might be at the other side? What might you *see*?

You *breathe* deeply, summoning up your courage.

You *must* open the door. You *feel* the prickles of perspiration on your forehead.

You grip the handle firmly. You *hold your breath*. Slowly . . . very, very slowly you turn the handle . . . and . . . you . . . open . . . the door.

As you do – something *brushes* against your leg.

Did you create any atmosphere? How did you do it? Notice that you *must not be in too much of a hurry* to reach the climax.

On the other hand, you must be careful not to drag out the scene too long so that the story loses interest.

For the following scenes you have been given only brief suggestions because now you should be able to work out your ideas quite competently. In each case work to create atmosphere – and use your senses. Perhaps it will be easier to mime the scenes first, adding dialogue later.

a A group of people are travelling on an aeroplane. Suddenly there is a reason for tension.

b You are enjoying a party until . . .

c A group of campers are about to settle down for the night when . . .

d Some people are trapped in a cave. The incoming tide is beginning to fill the cavern. The only way out appears to be through a very small hole in the roof.

e Haunted!

f Two explorers find themselves in swampland.

g Each member of a group has to cross a 'tightrope' which is stretched across a fast-flowing river.

Compose any piece of writing that is suggested by this photograph:

The ingredients of a story

Good stories, like good cakes, contain several 'ingredients'.

1 ACTION

People like a story to move, things to happen. If a tale is *only* talk it can so often become boring.

1 CHARACTERS

These should be as real as possible. Look again at the part of this book entitled 'People' (Chapter 2).

136

3 BACKGROUND

The characters have to act and speak. They must have somewhere to do this, so they must be given a background. The setting of a story might be in the Rocky Mountains of Canada, for example, or in a coal-mine, a doctor's surgery, a school, a building-site, a lawyer's office, the wide open prairies etc.

4 DESCRIPTION

Of course, the characters, the background and the action all require a certain amount of description. You must be careful to see that your description is vivid and not overdone, for too much can hold up the action and lead to boredom.

5 SUSPENSE

Every story must rise to a climax. The story should then end quickly. Before the climax is reached the author must keep his reader in suspense, making him wonder what will happen next.

6 DIALOGUE

This should be interesting, and it *must be necessary* to the story. It should help the action forward and/or help to reveal something about a character(s).

7 ATMOSPHERE

The writer should aim to create an atmosphere which is suitable to the kind of story being written.

Legends

One of our earliest type of story is the *legend*. Very often these tales were told, or sung, by wandering minstrels, and most were in verse form. Many of the stories concerned famous people and their deeds – deeds which were usually greatly exaggerated.

A very early story in our language, for example, was 'Beowulf'. In this the hero, Beowulf, fights a terrifying monster called Grendel – and he wounds it fatally. When we read it we do not believe the tale – but, nevertheless, it is a very good story.

Take Robin Hood, for example. Some people believe that he really existed. Some say he did not. Yet others think that he is a 'collection' of many men. Whatever the truth – the stories about him are very good and extremely popular.

Then there is King Arthur. Did he exist? If he did – where did he live? How much is true about him? Whatever the truth, as with Robin Hood, King Arthur and his Knights have provided us with some thrilling stories.

How did legends start?

Most legends are probably partly true, but much additional material is fictitious. Let us see how a legend *might* have originated – by taking a modern example:

Imagine that a girl – we will call her Jane – is cycling home from school one evening when, accidentally, she falls off the machine. She grazes her hand on a wall, but otherwise there is no damage. The next day, for some reason unconnected with the accident, she fails to turn up at school. Then someone remembers having seen Jane fall off her bicycle. She tells her friends – 'Did you know that Jane fell off her bike last night? I heard she broke her arm!'

One of the friends then tells *her* friend the tale – 'Jane ran into a wall on her bike. She cut herself ever so badly, and broke her arm. The bike's smashed!'

So the story goes on. By the time friend number two has told her friend the story has been exaggerated even more!

'Did you know that Jane was in a smash with a car? She's still unconscious. The car driver's in hospital, too.'

By the time the story has been narrated several more times poor Jane will have been involved in a major disaster.

Of course, that story has been greatly exaggerated, but you can probably see what is meant. What about the ancient legend? Imagine –

A man is going home across some dreary stretch of moorland when he is startled by the sudden appearance of a large fox. By the time the man arrives home the animal has grown (in his mind) into some terrible creature. When the incident is reported to his friends the fox has become a monster.

Tenses

Most stories, letters, diaries etc. are written in the past tense.

E.g. 'I *parked* the car and *walked* up the hill, feeling sure that I *was being followed*. Ahead of me I *saw* that the slope *was covered* by thick forest, and I *hurried* on. The moment I *entered* the safety of the trees I *glanced* back and *saw* something shining. I *knew* it *was* them . . .

Writing in the *present* tense can be difficult, but it can also be effective, especially to create atmosphere:

e.g. It must be nearly dawn now. The man, who has been standing near the cliff-tops during the past hours, is tiring. He leans heavily against the tree and his head droops towards his chest. If only he would sleep.

Carefully, almost afraid to breathe, fearing that the tiny sound is magnified by the night air, Linda raises herself on to her elbows and tries to pierce the gloom. Is he asleep? She thinks he might be.

For a long minute she remains poised. In order to reach safety she must cross more than fifty yards of open ground. Not a tree, not a bush, not even a rock offers any hope of concealment.

He *is* asleep. She feels sure of that now. Slowly, so slowly, she creeps her right hand forward. The dry grasses rustle as her fingers spread along the ground. She looks up. The man remains motionless. Her left hand steals forward, trembling. A knee is drawn up. Then the other. She moves, but no more than a few inches.

Again she glances up and sees, with dismay, the first russet streaks of dawn cracking the night sky. She cannot possibly reach the sanctuary of the ancient ruins before daylight will reveal her to the mysterious watcher.

Can you continue a paragraph which begins –
'The examination room is very hot and quiet'?

Mixing tenses for no good reason is a very common *mistake* with young writers. Very often pupils do not realise that they *have* mixed the tenses of the verbs – unless they read the passage aloud.

The following extract is taken from a short story. Sam has bought a house which is said to be haunted:

It was in the dark, mean hours of the early morning when Sam awoke suddenly. Something in the house had disturbed him.

Listen! A mouse-hunting owl moaned dismally in the nearby wood. A badger coughed. A hungry fox barked. But listen! Those were not the noises that caused Sam's skin to prickle.

'Lubb-dupp! Lubb-dupp!'

A strange sound, yet faintly familiar. He lay quiet, straining his ears until they almost hurt.

'Lubb-dupp! Lubb-dupp!'

It was his heart. Yes – his own heart beating, thumping, pounding his ribs. He put a cold hand on his chest. For a while he remained motionless. Then he recognised the sound. Not his heart! It was the noise made by someone breathing. Someone breathing heavily – regularly – horribly in the lonely darkness.

Sam held his breath. Perhaps it was himself. Perhaps he was still half asleep, hearing his own breathing magnified by the semi-stupor of near-sleep.

'Lubb-dupp!' Heavy. Regular.

Haunted! Surely it couldn't be that! But it seemed that it was. He sat up.

The breathing was still there, like the sound of a man gasping his last. It filled the room. It grew louder. Louder! Louder!

Sam leaped from the bed with a speed that surprised even himself. He rushed into the next room, holding his hands over his ears. He stopped, took away his hands and listened. It was there, too – pulsing, throbbing in the night.

Horrified, he tried every room in the house. The result was always the same. The breathing laboured everywhere. . . .

a Noises in the night often cause fear, but they are usually unexplained noises. Here some of the sounds *are* recognised, yet they frighten. What are they and why do they have such an effect?

b What effect has the word 'something' in the first paragraph?

c On which of the senses has the writer concentrated? Why has the sense of sight been neglected, apart from the fact that the story takes place at night?

d Which words, especially, contribute to the creation of 'atmosphere'? Why do they do so?

e What might the strange noise have been? Try to write the end of the story.

What kind of atmosphere is created in this passage?

A clock was tolling midnight as we approached the castle, a dark ruin, sinister under a starless night. We stopped and huddled close to a screen of thin trees which hid us from any watchers in the massive shell ahead. I shuddered as a lone owl, foraging in the rustling wood behind us, cried out, seemingly to warn us, though half-heartedly, to return whence we had come before it was too late. . . .

Which words in the extract *particularly* contribute to the creation of 'atmosphere'?

Another kind of atmosphere is created in this passage:

An old man, a very old man, moved slowly along the deck, gazing with dull eyes at the parched boards beneath him. Dry, dead, shrunken boards – and water to the furthest edge of the world. The ship was becalmed, had been becalmed for two long days. The man stopped and peered at a sailor, his one friend, who now lay motionless, his body partly shrouded by a ragged piece of ship' canvas. . . .

The next passage contains several ingredients which help to suggest atmosphere:

> Now the hungry lion roars,
> And the wolf behowls the moon;
> Whilst the heavy plowman snores,

All with weary task fordone.
Now the wasted brands do glow,
Whilst the screech-owl, screeching loud,
Puts the wretch that lies in woe
In remembrance of a shroud.
Now it is the time of night
That the graves, all gaping wide,
Every one lets forth his sprite,
In the churchway paths to glide:
And we fairies, that do run
By the triple Hecate's team
From the presence of the sun,
Following darkness like a dream,
Now are frolic; not a mouse
Shall disturb this hallowed house.

From *A Midsummer Night's Dream* by **William Shakespeare**.

a How is atmosphere created here?

b What are the 'brands' and why are they 'wasted'?

c About what is the 'wretch that lies in woe' probably dreaming?

d Why should the fairies run away from the sun?

e What might be seen gliding in the 'churchway paths'?

This next extract describes how a train is about to pass over a bridge. Notice how short is the line which contains the climax:

He was imprisoned in the train, which advanced inexorably, winding in its own glare like a dark red serpent twisting sinuously forward. It had traversed one mile of the bridge and had now reached the middle span, where a mesh of steel girders formed a hollow tube through which it must pass. The train entered this tunnel. It entered slowly, fearfully, reluctantly, juddering in every bolt and rivet of its frame as the hurricane assaulted, and sought to destroy, the greater resistance now offered to it. The wheels clanked with the ceaseless insistence of the tolling of a passing bell, still protesting endlessly:

'God help us! God help us! God help us!'

Then, abruptly, when the whole train lay enwrapped within the iron lamellae of the middle link of the bridge, the wind elevated itself with a culminating, exultant roar to the orgasm of its power and passion.

The bridge broke.

From *Hatter's Castle* by **A. J. Cronin**

a What one word in the first sentence sets the 'mood' of this extract?

b Why is the simile – 'like a dark red serpent' particularly apt here?

c The last sentence contains the climax. Why is it so effective?

d Why does the writer use the phrase 'the tolling of a passing bell'?

Write paragraphs – in the *present tense* – using the following as main sentences:

a It is dusk and all is very quiet.

b Breathlessly we watch as the man climbs slowly up the rock face.

c The interior of the coach is very hot and the passengers are becoming more and more irritable.

d The leaves protest loudly as the rising wind whips them along the gutters.

e Joan, being unused to tents, cannot sleep.

f The shopping crowds jostle the old man.

g It is still raining, though not so heavily.

h From this distance we can barely hear the sounds of harvesting in the fields far below.

i Bill is tired, and the motorway seems endless.

j Slowly the huge balloon lifts into the clear sky.

Now re-write each of your paragraphs – but in the *past tense*.

Imagination

'Use your imagination'.

That has probably been said to you often, but what does it really mean? Read this extract:

Without speaking he seized my arms and forced them behind me. Then, quickly and efficiently, he tied my hands together. I wanted to cry out as the rough rope dragged the skin from my wrists as he twisted and pulled. When he had bound me securely he placed his foot against my back and heaved me forward. I saw the jagged stones rush towards my face as I fell. . . .

We can *imagine* that scene. We can *imagine* the ropes rubbing away the soft skin of the wrists. We can *imagine* the feeling of horror that he experienced as he fell forwards, his face completely unprotected.

That is not the only way in which our imaginations work, however. We must call upon our imaginations to help us to write. Read the following extract from a story:

At last the holidays had arrived and I was on my way, heading for the little market town in South Wales, the town where I was born and to which I often return. On this particular trip I was driving a car which I had borrowed from a friend. It was a gentle summer evening. The air was balmy and the dusk was softly shrouding the lovely countryside.

Having driven for many miles, I decided, when about five miles from my home, to take a short-cut, a short-cut I had frequently taken when I was a boy.

But – things change!

Within minutes I had lost myself in a maze of country lanes and then – it had to happen – I ran out of petrol, right on the edge of an immense stretch of woodland ... and it was growing dark rapidly.

What was I to do? There was but one thing I could do. I locked the car and began to walk, hoping, I suppose, either to find a garage or my home. I found neither.

Gradually, the lane that I was following grew narrower until it became hardly more than a path. The night was growing darker.

Very soon I was deep in the wood. It was now so dark that I could see barely a yard in front of me.

I began to be aware of strange patterings and rustlings around me, and I was nervous. Then I saw, far in front of me, a light. Someone's cottage, I thought, but there – in the middle of a wood in the Twentieth Century? No – it was not a cottage, I concluded.

The light was bigger now, and it glowed like a fire. Of course! That was it. The light was a fire. But whose? In a place like this?

I hurried towards the glow, which grew larger with each step I took. The fire – for that was what it proved to be – was in the centre of a clearing amongst the trees. It was inviting, despite the warmth of the evening. I was about to stride into the clearing when something, instinct, perhaps, stopped me. Whose fire was it? There was no one there. At least, I could see no one.

Suddenly ...

That story has been left unfinished for the reason that it had no end. In fact, it never really happened – not all of it. The writer *did* take a short-cut and he *did* run out of petrol and he *did* set off to find a garage, but there the real story ends. From that point the writer allowed his imagination to take over. 'What *might* have happened if I had gone into the wood and lost myself?' was the question he asked himself. Other questions followed.

You might like to try to invent an end to that story. Keep asking yourself – 'What if ... ?'

We are frequently told that if we wish to write we should write about things that we know. That is very good advice, but there are times when we want to write about things that we do not know – when we want to use our imaginations. If authors did not do so we should have no Science Fiction or murder stories, for example. The authors have to use their imaginations.

Read these paragraphs:

a Last night heavy rain flooded the town of Redfern. High winds damaged roofs and felled trees in the surrounding countryside.

b Last night Redfern looked like a ghost-town, deserted, dead! Throughout the afternoon and evening a river of foul-smelling water rushed unchecked through the narrow streets. Slates, from a hundred roofs, hurled themselves into the swirling mass, while above, in a leaden sky, ragged clouds moved heavily.

Passage (a) states facts.

Passage (b) attempts to paint a picture for the reader.

Here are two more passages, one 'fact' and the other 'fiction'.

a The convict was recaptured last night. He had hidden amongst the rocks of Facefell Moors. He looked tired and hungry and he offered no resistance when arrested.

b Suddenly we were aware of the rustling of the ferns ahead of us. John nudged me, signalling me to lie still and keep quiet. I looked towards the rocks in front of us, where a face had appeared, an evil-looking face, blackened by the weather and by a thickening growth of three days' beard. The tiny eyes, made even more minute by the puffiness about them, seemed to bore through the gloom . . .

Now see what you can achieve as 'word artists'. Read the following statements of facts and then try to create a vivid word picture of each. Imagine that each passage you write is part of a story.

a Snow fell again last night, the heaviest fall since records began.

b High seas have made it impossible for the supply ship to deliver Christmas goods to the Outsea Light-house.

c Eye-witnesses have stated that a 'saucer-like object' landed in Churnley Wood last night.

d The explorers said that heat and thirst almost killed them when they were crossing the desert.

e The fine weather has encouraged many people to visit the new fun-fair at Lough-on-Sea.

f Read what you can about the following. Then write – (i) a factual account and (ii) a passage of fiction about each:

a cowboys	b highwaymen	c smugglers
d lifeboats	e firemen	f deserts
g ghosts	h crocodiles	i skiing
j oil-rigs	k policemen	l hurricanes

m windmills	n earthquakes	o show-jumping
p vampires	q tea-clippers	r hot-air balloons
s light-houses	t motor grand-prix	

Figurative Language

Similes

Writers often use decorative – or figurative – language to help them create vivid pictures. A favourite device is a *simile*.

E.g. Rain dripped from the flowers like tear-drops.

Here the writer feels that the rain drops look like tears. They are *similar* to tears in appearance. Therefore he employs a phrase which is known as a *simile* – like tear-drops.

Look at another example:

Her hands were as rough as the rotting concrete on the quay.

The words underlined form another *simile* because the roughness of her hands is *similar* to the roughness of the concrete.

There are scores of ready-made similes in existence:

The night was as dark as pitch.
The old house was as silent as a tomb.
She ran like the wind.
The little boy was as happy as a king.
The girl sang like a lark.
The old man was as deaf as a post.
The newly-washed sheet was as white as snow.
Alison and Ted sat in the room as quiet as mice.
The water in the pool was as clear as day.
Suddenly he awoke, feeling as cold as ice.
They told Terry that the old woman was as wise as an owl.
Mr Jones, the blacksmith, was as strong as an ox.

Those similes are quite good. In fact, they were very good when they were written originally. They have been used so frequently, however, that they have lost most of their value. Rewrite the above sentences, making up your own similes – ones that are fresh and imaginative.

Complete the following sentences by using suitable similes. Avoid those that are ready-made:

a After a cold night the frost lay on the ground like ....
b Suddenly the man jumped into the sea as ....
c The lake lay in the moonlight as...................................
d John rushed off down the road as..................................

e All day the rain fell like ....
f As Emma walked along the gloomy drive she began to tremble
like...
g The flowers in the park were like ....
h We remembered the Bank Holiday because the heat was like ..
i As the motor-cycle rounded the bend its engine roared like....
j The kitten was fluffy like...

Write ten sentences of your own, each to include a fresh and
imaginative simile.

Metaphors

Another favourite device of the writer is the use of what is known
as a *metaphor*. Again, this is a phrase where two things are
compared, but this time the words 'like' or 'as' are not used. Instead
– the one thing is said *to be* the other.

E.g. The boxer was a real lion in the fight.

Of course, he was *not* a real lion. He simply fought as bravely
and as fiercely as a real lion.

Take another example:

The singer said that if his girl-friend left him she would
break his heart.

She will make him sad, perhaps, but she will not really break his
heart, will she?

The phrases underlined in the above examples are *metaphors*.

As with similes, so with *metaphors*. There are dozens ready-
made and over-worked:

He is a wet blanket.
Mr Jones is a jack-of-all-trades.
It was my task to pour oil on troubled waters.
The argument between Mary and her sister was no more than
a storm in a teacup.
Two days later they decided to bury the hatchet.
The news of the attack was a bolt from the blue.
We could place no value on the opinion of Mr Williams who had
an axe to grind.
The other boys teased Matthew, saying that he was tied to his
mother's apron-strings.
Nicola was a dreamer, always building castles in the air.
The children were never afraid of the old man for they knew that
his bark was worse than his bite.
Being unable to keep a secret, Karen soon let the cat out of the bag.
Keith told them that as the damage had already been done there
was no point in crying over spilt milk.

The words underlined in the above examples are well-worn metaphorical expressions. Rewrite the sentences, using plain English in place of the metaphorical expressions.

Discover the origins of the following metaphorical phrases and then write a brief account of each, giving their meanings:

a an Achilles heel.
b a Job's comforter.
c to send to Coventry.
d a good Samaritan.
e to cut the Gordian knot.
f a pig in a poke.
g a Quixotic person.
h a red-letter day.
i to bell the cat.
j a Cadmean victory.
k sailing under false colours.
l to draw the long bow.
m to wear Hector's cloak.
n the Midas touch.
o to kill the fatted calf.
p a turncoat.
q the writing on the wall.
r to strike while the iron's hot.
s on the nail.
t to make bricks without straw.

Rewrite the following sentences so that the metaphorical expressions are *explained*.

E.g. The Mayor *struck at the root of the trouble*.

That *is* a sentence, but its meaning is not clear. It might be written –

> Having ordered the hungry citizens to be fed, the Mayor was confident that there would be no more rioting, believing that he had struck at the root of the trouble.

a John was definitely a fair-weather sailor.
b The police combed the area where the robbery had taken place.
c Harry found himself taking a busman's holiday.
d Old Mr Jones was a Scrooge.
e Joy regretted resting on her laurels.
f Bill's friends said that he was a bull in a china shop.
g Mr Smith was one of the old school.
h Eric had feet of clay.
i Jim was well-known for blowing his own trumpet.
j The family barely kept the wolf from the door.

More Paragraphs

Remember: *one* main idea – *one* paragraph.

Write about the following, taking care to break up your work into correct paragraphs. Some suggestions are offered for the first three:

a *Myself*
  Paragraph 1 .... personal details (age, height etc.)
  Paragraph 2 .... hobbies
  Paragraph 3 .... things I like/dislike

b *Our school*
  Paragraph 1 .... the outside appearance
  Paragraph 2 .... the interior
  Paragraph 3 .... the staff
  Paragraph 4 .... subjects taught

c *Hobbies*
  Paragraph 1 .... why I took it up
  Paragraph 2 .... simple beginnings
  Paragraph 3 .... the 'expert'
  Paragraph 4 .... costs
  Paragraph 5 .... the value of a good hobby

d I like being young because...

e Saturdays in our house...

f The day I took charge ....

g Things I dislike ....

h A journey I enjoyed ....

i My family...

j Our village ....

k My bicycle is old, but...

l Our new teacher ....

m The old vicarage ....

n Near our house is a derelict warehouse ....

o The canal was no longer used.......................................

p The adventure playground ....

q We went into the musty-smelling shop.............................

r The new house...

s When we arrived at the safari-park ....

t My first trip by rail...

Compose any pieces of writing suggested by these quotations:

a Animals are such agreeable friends.
       George Eliot

b St. Agnes' Eve – Ah, bitter chill it was!
    The owl, for all his feathers, was a-cold;
    The hare limped trembling through the frozen grass,
    And silent was the flock in woolly fold.
    From *The Eve of St. Agnes* by **John Keats**

c I am monarch of all I survey,
    My right there is none to dispute;
    From the centre all round to the sea,

I am lord of the fowl and the brute.
From *Alexander Selkirk* by **William Cowper**

d It was a summer evening,
  Old Kasper's work was done,
  And he before his cottage door
  Was sitting in the sun.
        Robert Southey

Compose any piece of writing that is suggested to you by this photograph:

Re-read the advice on 'Formal Reports' on p. 57 and then compile the following:

Individual or group work

a Carry out a survey amongst the pupils in your school, asking questions about the types of pets they own. Discover how they feed them, house them, exercise them, and what arrangements are made for them when the owners go away on holiday. Present your findings and conclusions in the form of a written report.

b Imagine that you have been asked by a company to test a new fountain-pen for them before it is offered on general sale. You should note such points as: the ease with which the ink flows, the smoothness of writing, the 'comfort' of the implement in the fingers, the quality of the barrel and the nib, the ease of filling, the suitability of the clip and the proposed price. Submit your findings to the company in a concise, but detailed report.

c By making use of the reference books in your school and/or local library, learn what you can about hospitals since the Middle Ages. Having done so, write a report that is to be delivered at a 'Speakers' Club'.

d Learn what you can about the canals of Britain, their building, administration, use, their loss of commercial popularity and efforts to revive them. Write a clear, detailed report as a result of your research.

e Fashions in clothes, furniture, holidays, entertainments and travel have altered considerably during the past century. When you have discovered all you can about such changes write a detailed and, perhaps, illustrated, report about your findings.

f Write a report in which you trace the progress made in the provision, building, organisation and administration of schools in this country since the Middle Ages.

g Invent a large new housing-estate and then 'interview' the people you intend to live there, asking them what shops, places of entertainment and other facilities they think will be necessary. Having done so, submit your findings as a report to the local council.

h Conduct a survey in your school, aiming to discover the types of holidays preferred by the pupils. Write your findings and conclusions in the form of a report.

i Study the chart opposite and then write a clear report, explaining your observations and deductions.

j Carry out a school survey, discovering television programmes that are popular and unpopular with the pupils and their parents. Write out your observations and deductions in the form of a report.

k Write a clear, concise report of an experiment that you have completed in a science lesson.

l Write a report on an article (e.g. a bicycle, a washing-machine, a record-player etc) that you wish to sell.

m Compose a school report on yourself as it might be written by – (i) your teacher and (ii) yourself.

n Write a report, which is to be presented to the Headteacher of the school, on a recent field-trip or study weekend enjoyed by a group of pupils.

o Write a report on the arrangements made to hold the school examinations. Add comments of your own, pointing out where you think improvements might be made.

Accidents

Age group	Struck by vehicles	Car drivers	Motor cycle drivers	Accidents in the home
0–5 yrs	4	0	0	37
6–11 yrs	26	0	0	24
12–15 yrs	13	0	0	8
16–20 yrs	9	21	56	2
21–26 yrs	6	36	21	2
32–50 yrs	4	28	3	12
Over 60 yrs	14	18	1	39

p Having carried out a survey into the types of sporting activities preferred by the pupils in your school, sum up your findings in a written report.

q Imagine that your neighbourhood has suffered severe damage during a fierce gale. Describe the devastation in the form of a written report which is to be presented to the local authority.

r Consider how you have spent your leisure-time during the past year and write a report on your findings. Add some thoughtful comments.

s Your school or club has held a Christmas Fayre and Social. Write a report on its success (or failure) and mention improvements that might be made for the next year.

t Write a report, describing the progress made in the past fifty years in one of the following (or all, if you wish) forms of transport.
(*i*) road (*ii*) rail (*iii*) air (*iv*) water

Dialogues

Remember: When writing dialogue:
Write only what is interesting and/or informative.

Use contracted forms (i.e. can't; we'll etc.) where it will add realism to the conversation.

Be sure that facts used are correct.

Try to reveal something of the character through his/her conversation.

Invent interesting and worthwhile pieces of dialogue between:

a You and a Martian who has just landed on a lonely moor.
b You and the Snow Queen when you wander into her palace.
c Two witches in a forest.
d Two friends at a Christmas party.
e Two sailors adrift in an open boat.
f Two explorers in the jungle.
g Two friends who are lost in an underground cavern.
h A postman and a householder after a night of storms.
i A fireman and his wife after he has attended a farm fire.
j A trapped pot-holer and a member of a rescue-team.
k Yourself and a very small child during a visit to a farm or zoo.
l You and a very old superstitious man who sees in the weather 'signs of trouble to come'.
m A telephone conversation between you and a friend who is away on holiday.
n A Customs Officer and a traveller.
o An air-hostess and a nervous passenger.
p A hairdresser and a customer.
q A policeman and a lost child.
r A teenager and a centenarian.
s A bread roundsman and a customer with a complaint.
t Yourself and a shop-keeper when you do not know the name of the item you wish to buy, but you can describe it.

Compose any piece of writing that is suggested by the photograph on the opposite page.

Panel Discussions

Group, or class, discussions are valuable in that they give pupils opportunities to offer their own opinions on various topics and also to hear those of others. Interchanging ideas orally can also assist you to discuss problems in writing to produce what is sometimes known as an 'argumentative' essay!

A panel discussion is another method of dealing with a problem. Here a group of people, each having a particular interest in a certain topic, meet together to talk about it.

E.g. Topic: Fashions in clothes.
     Panel: A clothing manufacturer; a teenage girl; a teenage boy; a mother; a father; a shopkeeper; a teacher.

Form your own panels and discuss the following topics. The members of the panels for the first two are suggested, but you may change them, of course. It is up to you to decide who will take part in the rest.

a Topic: Holidays are un-necessary.
    Panel: A seaside landlady; a child; a parent; a travel agent; a resident from a holiday resort; the manager of a holiday camp; the proprietor of a camping-site.

b Topic: Pupils should not be allowed to work out of school.
    Panel: A shop-keeper; a teacher; two pupils; a policeman; a husband and wife; a parent from a one-parent family.

c Topic: Violence on television affects us all.

d Topic: There is no true sport.

e Topic: Discipline! Who is responsible?

f Topic: School uniform is a thing of the past.

g Topic: Road accidents *will* happen.

h Topic: The problem of litter is for the Government to solve.

i Topic: Vandalism is everybody's business.

j Topic: Homework is quite un-necessary.

k Topic: We can live without motorways.

l Topic: Good manners have no place in our lives today.

m Topic: The planning of our living communities is the main cause of boredom in young people.

n Topic: People who indulge in dangerous pastimes, such as rock-climbing or pot-holing, are selfish. They gain nothing but personal satisfaction and put others at risk.

o Topic: If a mother has to go out to work, her husband should make himself responsible for half the housework.

Stories

Remember that when you write a story you should aim to capture the interest of your reader *at once*.

E.g. Title: *An Exciting Holiday Incident*.

A long introduction explaining how you decided to take a holiday in Cornwall and your journey there is quite un-necessary. Doing so is likely to bore your reader. Try to create suspense immediately:

It was on the second night of our Cornish holiday that the strange man appeared . . .

or I had always believed that smugglers in Cornwall were beings of the past . . . until I walked along a lonely beach on that warm August evening. . . .

or 'Quick – down!' whispered Peter.

The two boys dropped into the soft grass and peered through the gloom.

'*They* are not holiday-makers, I know,' muttered Tom.

Write stories suggested by:

a Found!

b Alone!

c Fire Aboard!

d The First Snow.

e A Walk On An Autumn Afternoon.

f Christmas Afternoon At Home.

g A Terrifying Night.

h The Night The Martians Landed.

i Winter Evenings.

j An Afternoon At The Seaside.

k Write a story in which you have to cross a river which is in flood.

l One day you are visiting a zoo when a monkey escapes.

m Write a story concerning the supernatural.

n Write a story in which some violent 'outrage of nature' – such as an avalanche, a thunderstorm, a volcano etc. actually comes to your aid.

o A group of friends go swimming in a lake when one of them gets into difficulties.

Write stories which begin:

a Black clouds drifted across the moon ....

b It was the first white Christmas I could remember..............

c We had just begun our holidays ....

d It had been such a hot day. Who could have guessed that such a night could have followed?

e I wish I had never seen the thing...............................

f I shall never forget that Sunday night ....

g 'What do you think this is?' asked John.

h Having parked his car, the strange man set off across the heath, glancing behind him at every step ....

i At first I did not realise that it was a fire.......................

j We had never believed Mary until................................

Write stories which end:

a ....and that was the last time we saw him.

b ....so who says there is no such thing as luck?

c ....from that day the old man was kind and gentle to everyone.

d.........she has never found the key to that door.

e.........and they proved to be real after all.

Write a story:

a Which includes – a castle; a wood; danger; escape.

b Which includes – a milkman; a letter; a reward.

c Which includes – a pool; friends having a picnic; a dog.

d Which includes – a bicycle; a stream; wind.

e Which includes – two friends; a quarrel; an accident.

f Which includes – a coach; a safari-park; photographs; a competition.

g Which includes – Christmas; a class-room; a misunderstanding.

h Which includes – a large shop; a small child; a parent.

i Which includes – a lost fountain-pen; accusations; a teacher.

j Which inclues – a fire; an old lady; two young friends.

Compose any piece of writing that is suggested to you by this photograph:

Diaries

Using your imagination, write diaries for the following:

a Yourself – including –
   a winter week; a spring week; an autumn week; a summer week.
b A mountaineer.
c Explorers who are trying to contact a little-known tribe.
d Your friend.
e Anyone of your choice.
f A reporter on (*i*) a national newspaper, (*ii*) a local newspaper.
g The proprietor of a market stall.
h A pot-holer.
i A cricketer.
j A church caretaker.
k A door-to-door salesman.
l A motorway patrol policeman.
m A beach deck-chair attendant.
n The groundsman of a football club.

o Someone living at the top of a high block of flats.
p A hairdresser.
q A street-photographer at a seaside resort.
r An actor/actress.
s Someone working at a safari-park.
t A long-distance coach driver.

Look at the sketch-map on p. 158 of a large park in a city. Although it might be a pleasant place, it is very badly planned.

For example,

The car-park, being at the side of a busy dual-carriageway, is likely to cause traffic problems, especially at holiday periods, when hundreds of vehicles might be moving along the road while others are trying to enter or leave the park.

a In what other ways do you think the layout of the park shows thoughtless planning? Give reasons for your answers.

b Imagine that you have been given unlimited funds and the opportunity to begin again. Describe how you would reorganise the park sensibly, giving reasons for your decisions. (Although this question asks what you *would* do – it might be advisable to write your answer in the *past tense*, as if you have already completed the project. Otherwise you will probably find that you have to repeat the word 'would' so frequently that your composition will sound ugly when read.)

c Describe how you spent an afternoon in the park as if you were:
   an elderly person.
   a child.
   a first-aid officer.
   a sports enthusiast.
   a park attendant.
   Each of the above will, obviously, spend time in an area in which he/she is particularly interested. For example, the child will go to the playground, and the sports enthusiast will probably play golf.
   Try to make the afternoon for each person varied and interesting. You might also mention such things as the weather, the quality of the equipment, and the condition of the park.

d Imagine that you live in one of the houses along the side of the park in Leaf Crescent:
   (*i*) Describe the view as you look out of your front window early on a summer morning.
   (*ii*) Describe the view during a Bank Holiday afternoon.

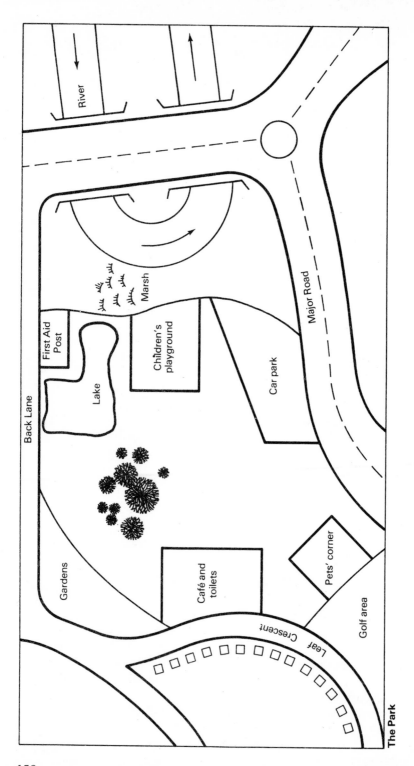

The Park

e Write a letter to the Parks Department, complaining about the amount of litter left in the park during the weekend.

f Write an article for a local newspaper, describing the advantages and disadvantages of living in a house that overlooks a popular park.

g Imagine that you are the Superintendant in charge of the city's parks. Write a letter to the Editor of the local newspaper, making your own observations about the behaviour of some people using the parks.

Interviews

Remember: when writing an interview be sure that you have something to say and that the facts stated are correct.

Read the following extract from an interview between a newspaper reporter and a man who has just returned from an expedition in South America.

REPORTER Well, Mr Sampson, what does it feel like to be back in England?

SAMSON Fine.

REPORTER Does this cold weather suit you?

SAMSON Not very much.

REPORTER Where are you going to spend Christmas?

SAMSON I'm going down to London to stay with friends.

REPORTER You'll have a lot to tell them I suppose?

SAMSON Oh, yes. I haven't seen them for some time.

REPORTER It should be an enjoyable time for all of you, then? Thank you and good luck, Mr Samson.

Mr Samson might have a 'lot to tell his friends', but he certainly did not tell us much. The Reporter's questions, of course, were not very constructive. Almost anyone, whether he had been to South America or not, could have answered *those* questions.

The interview might have started like this, for example:

REPORTER Welcome home, Mr Samson. How does it feel to be back in England after an absence of two years?

SAMSON Fine! The cold weather is not so pleasant, though, after the blazing sun of South America.

REPORTER Did you make any interesting discoveries while you were there?

SAMSON We came across a tribe of people who had never before seen anyone like us.

REPORTER Were they friendly?

SAMSON Not at first. They were quite frightening. Luckily they became fascinated by our cameras, and gradually they grew almost friendly. We, in turn, were amazed when we saw their 'houses'.

REPORTER Would you like to tell me about them?

SAMSON Indeed I would. In the thickest part of the jungle . . .

a Read about the following places and the people who live there. Make notes of any interesting facts and then write interviews between a reporter and someone who has just returned from: Holland; Canada; Egypt; The Bahamas; China.

b Write an interview between an Earth visitor who has landed on Mars and one of the 'inhabitants' of the planet.

You will have to do a good deal of research before attempting the following 'interviews'.

c Write interviews between a young person who is interested in a career in one of the following trades or professions and an expert in each particular field:
medicine; science; hairdressing; air-hostess; flying; journalism; sales-person; space science; missionary work; veterinary work; rescue work; police; teaching; writing; theatre; television; local government; furniture manufacture.

d Write interviews between a member of the public and a volunteer worker in:
The British Red Cross Society; The St. John's Ambulance Brigade; the nursing world; work with old people; work with deprived people.

e Write interviews between a newspaper reporter and someone who has been involved in a disaster such as:
floods: a hurricane; a volcano; a fire; a blizzard; an earthquake; a shipwreck; an air-crash.

f Write interviews between yourself and a famous character from a book or a play, such as:
Tom the Chimney-sweep; Oliver Twist; Snow White; David Copperfield; Jane Eyre.

g Write interviews between a reporter and someone from the past:
e.g. Florence Nightingale; Henry the Fifth; Louis Pasteur; George Stevenson; Charles Dickens; Dr. Livingstone.

h Write interviews, which are to be published in the school magazine, with:
a clergyman; a farmer; a surgeon; the Editor of a newspaper; a professional footballer; an actor/actress.

i Write interviews between a reporter and someone who has had

160

an unusual experience:

e.g. Someone who has been rescued from a pot-hole; a diver who has been threatened by an underwater creature; a person who has had to bale out of an aeroplane.

j Write a real interview between yourself and one of your teachers.

Speeches

At some time you have probably had to listen to a speech which has bored you. There could be several reasons why that happened. Amongst the most common are the following:

1 The speaker's voice is monotonous.
2 He is concerned with using 'effective' words.
3 The speech is too long.
4 The speaker is talking about something that you cannot understand.
5 You cannot hear the speech clearly.
6 The speaker fidgets while he is talking.
7 The speaker does not know his subject thoroughly.
8 The speaker shouts, or whispers.
9 The speaker lacks confidence.

Having noted the above points and looked up the necessary information, write the following speeches and then deliver them to an audience:

a coin collecting.
b Achilles.
c moon landings.
d national emblems.
e Joseph Lister.
f animals of Africa.
g The Industrial Revolution.
h The Fleet Prison.
i Penicillin.
j Hovercraft.
k dairy-farming.
l Show-jumping as a spectator sport.
m advertisements.
n holidays at home.
o public transport.
p tourists.
q fun-fairs.
r rare birds.
s coast-guards.
t painting in oils.

Composition

a You return home very late from school, your shoes scuffed and your jacket torn. Write down the explanation you offered your parents and describe their reactions.

b While you are walking in the street you see a young child attempting to pull up a tiny sapling that has recently been planted. Write an account of the action you take. As you are older than the child you would be expected to behave in a responsible manner.

c Write a detailed description of the inside of your garage at home.

d Describe how you imagine the adult world appears to a small child.

e While journeying home during the evening rush-hour your 'bus is involved in a serious traffic-jam. Explain what happens, and describe your feelings, especially as you were in a particular hurry that day.

f Describe the working of any club or society with which you are involved at school.

g 'Our Welfare State is abused.' Write a composition in which you give your opinion of the statement quoted above.

h Write an account of a day in the life of a Roman soldier.

i Describe the work of three or four people whose occupations expose them to actual danger.

j Write a character-sketch of yourself as seen
  (*i*) by your parents.
  (*ii*) by your teacher.
  (*iii*) by yourself.

k Imagine that you have just retired from your life's work. Write your memoirs as if you had been:
  a fireman; a policeman; a farmer; a traffic-warden; a nurse; a teacher; a long-distance lorry-driver; a 'bus driver; a shop assistant; a postman.

l Write about your experiences when you worked during the holidays:
  a filling the shelves at a super-market.
  b as a waitress in a cafe.
  c assisting a park-keeper.
  d at a swimming-baths.
  e hay-making on a local farm.
  f running errands for the staff and the patients at the hospital.
  g at a garage.
  h in a book shop.
  i anywhere of your own choosing.

m 'It was different when I was young.' Imagine that you are an eighty-year-old grand-parent. Write an account of what you said to your grand-children to illustrate the above quotation.

162

n Write colourful descriptions of:
  (*i*) The scene in a harvest field.
  (*ii*) A horticultural show.
  (*iii*) A fashion parade.
o Guess who? Write a character-sketch of a member of the teaching staff without mentioning his/her name.
p Describe a scene of desolation, such as a piece of common land which is used as a rubbish-tip; a derelict coalmine; a stretch of windswept moorland.
q Describe a picnic spot as it appears on a warm, sunny day.

Projects

Group work

Working in groups, produce projects suggested by the following. Present your completed works in folders and try to include written reports, sketches, maps, plans, letters, diaries, anecdotes, written interviews (and/or tape-recorded ones), poems, charts, photographs, and illustrations.

a Vandalism! Hooliganism! Crime! Such items fill our newspapers day after day. Present a written project which shows that the great majority of young people are considerate, worthwhile citizens. For example, compose newspaper reports of charity schemes and community service. Write articles, reports and letters describing incidents of courage, effort, endurance, ingenuity, skill, sportsmanship. Invent a television documentary film. Record interviews.

b Invent an area of unpopulated land where a group of people, who are tired of the rush and bustle of modern life, settle. You might include reports on progress made, letters to relatives, plans and sketches, descriptions of the new living quarters, details of finding and growing food, stories of incidents that occur.

c People who serve the community! For example, milkmen; policemen; refuse-collectors; ambulance drivers; postmen. You might include written descriptions of the work done, diaries kept by some of the people, stories concerning them, talks given by them to other members of the community, interviews between them and reporters, news items.

d Conduct a survey amongst your friends, discovering the kinds of entertainment they enjoy. Present your findings and opinions in a written folder.

e By making use of reference books, to be found in your school library or at the local library, learn what you can about the 'homes of man' since earliest times. Having done so, make up an interesting, illustrated project, including descriptions, reports, diaries etc.

f Health is a major concern of everyone today, but it was not always so. Learn what you can about doctors, medicine and hospitals since medieval times. When you have done so present your findings in a well-written file.

g Animals. Present a well-written and well-illustrated project dealing with animals. You might include animals as pets, animals that work for man, performing animals, animals in captivity.

h Birds. Here you might include pet birds, birds of prey, working birds (such as racing pigeons, falcons), rare birds and extinct birds.

i Space. This project should stimulate your imaginations. For instance, you might imagine yourself actually on a new planet. How did you get there? How are you living? Is it already inhabited? What are the 'people' like?

j Your school wishes to raise a large amount of money to pay for a guide-dog for a blind person. Present a project in which you show, for example, letters written to various people seeking their support, reports of functions held, interviews, a television documentary.

k My autobiography. Write your autobiography and illustrate it with photographs, certificates, school reports etc. If you split it into four parts you will find it easier to manage. The following is a suggested plan:
Part 1 Early childhood. (Parents might help here)
Part 2 Infant and junior school days.
Part 3 Senior school days.
Part 4 Outside interests.

l A holiday brochure. Choose four types of holidays (for example, camping, walking tours, cycling holidays, boating holidays) and make up a holiday brochure, dealing with one type of holiday in each part. The places mentioned should be fictitious, but you can use pictures of real places. A typical plan might be:
Part 1 Holidays by the sea.
Part 2 Holidays in the country.
Part 3 Camping holidays.
Part 4 Hill-climbing holidays.

m Our village. Create a village in your mind and then write about it. You might find pictures with which to illustrate your work.

Maps and sketches might also be useful. A suggested plan might be:

Part 1 The village (with a map).
Part 2 Characters in the village.
Part 3 The 'history' of the village.
Part 4 Why I like (or dislike) living in the village.

n My magazine. This project might take a term to complete. Perhaps some of your weekly written work might be included. The following are some suggestions:

a Stories written by you.
b Poems written by you.
c Accounts of school visits made.
d Accounts of your hobbies, clubs.
e Sketches made by you.
f A cross-word and other puzzles invented by you.
g Letters to the Editor, and answers from the Editor.
h Your opinions on books and plays.
i Your opinions on various topics.

Individual written work

a Write a story, describing what happened the night some strange noises woke you.

b The Night the Police Called! Explain why they arrived and what happened.

c Write the opening chapter of a novel, setting the scene and introducing one main character.

d Write the first chapter of a novel in which the hero is a milkman.

e Describe how you spent a day at each of the following places of work: an office; a bank; a shop; a factory; a farm. Say which of the experiences you preferred and why. (You are not required to include any technical details. Simply describe what you *imagine* life is like in such places.)

f Begin a novel which is set in a hospital and introduce two characters.

g The City by Night! Write a story suggested by that title.

h Write a list of rules necessary for a party of children going to spend a day at the seaside. Give reasons for each.

i Write the opening chapter of a novel which is set on a farm.

j Make a list of rules necessary for the safe administration of (*i*) the Home Economics Department, (*ii*) the Woodwork/ Metalwork Departments of a school. Give reasons.

TOPIC INDEX